Designs
for the Contemporary
Woodworker

Designs
for the Contemporary
Woodworker

Richard M. Feldman

Illustrations by Robert Torre
Photographs by James Boorn

SAN DIEGO • NEW YORK
A. S. BARNES & COMPANY, INC.
IN LONDON:
THE TANTIVY PRESS

Designs for the Contemporary Woodworker
text copyright © 1980 by
A. S. Barnes and Co., Inc.

The Tantivy Press
Magdalen House
136-148 Tooley Street
London, SE1 2TT, England

First Edition
Manufactured in the United States of America
For information write to A. S. Barnes and Company, Inc.
P.O. Box 3051, San Diego, CA 92038

Library of Congress Cataloging in Publication Data

Feldman, Richard M.   1936-
   Designs for the contemporary woodworker.

   Bibliography: p.
   Includes index.
   1. Woodwork. I. Title.
TT180.F45   1980   684'.08   78-75311
ISBN 0-498-02314-1

1 2 3 4 5 6 7 8 9   84 83 82 81 80

To my wife,
Francine,
who is always a source of inspiration
and encouragement in any undertaking,
and to my daughters, Sabra and Hillary

Contents

Preface

The idea for writing this book materialized after noting how few books on modern design were available. Those designs appearing in the popular press were mostly traditional in style or amateurish in concept.

The projects in the second section are all wood and reflect the Danish influence as well as the American. They should each be viewed as a basic design, which may be altered to suit the needs and tastes of the individual as to form and function.

Construction is either of solid wood, wood veneer, or a combination of both. Veneers offer an exciting challenge, since they may be matched for interesting effect. Veneers are also cut from the choicest wood, so they have more beautiful colors and figures than solid lumber.

The chapters on construction, finishing, and the techniques of working with veneers are intentionally simplified, because publications are available on these subjects for the more advanced craftsman.

I hope that the projects presented will be as challenging for the beginner as well as the advanced craftsman, as they have been for me.

Acknowledgments

I wish to acknowledge the efforts of the following people, who have helped immeasurably, in preparing my manuscript and providing encouragement in this endeavor.

I am grateful to Eugene Grenz, my friend and attorney, who encouraged me to write this book and provided immeasurable legal assistance. Thanks is also due to Melanie Collins, who typed my manuscript, to Jason Maltz, who photocopied numerous pages of drawings, and to Patricia Becker, who assisted with some photography. Special thanks to my wife, Francine, whose encouragement, advice, and ideas led to the successful completion of this work.

R.M.F.

PART I
Design and Construction

1
Project Design

When viewing each design in the second section of this book do not consider it as a final statement. Most of these projects were only built after painstaking hours at the drawing board and many changes during construction.

Consider a flat surface in a design such as a jewelry box. The surface on the side of the box could be made broadly concave in cross section, a broad *V,* or convex. Of course some of these shapes would require solid and thicker wood for the side instead of veneers. Curves could be veneered providing they are not compound.

With the broad spectrum of colors and contrasts available in natural hardwoods, contrasting or complementary colors may be used for interest within a project.

Where a project is functional as well as decorative, think of its use before building. A lamp the proper height for an end table is not the proper height for a desk for good lighting. A serving tray will look beautiful with an oiled finish but will not stain when finished with one of the newer waterproof and alcohol-proof varnishes or sealers.

In designing your own projects or altering those shown, it is best to keep in mind that wooden design owes its beauty to simple form and clean uncluttered lines. Flat and broadly sculpted surfaces are unique. Mouldings and ornateness are to be strictly avoided. Decora-

15

tion is achieved through the use of the wood's color and natural markings in conjunction with simple form.

Construction considerations are of utmost importance in design. A well-designed piece which will not last with use serves no purpose. One should design items intended for heavy use strong enough to withstand that use.

2
Materials and Equipment

The materials used in these projects are solid hardwoods and softwoods and hardwood veneers. Solid hardwoods of the more common varieties such as birch, maple, walnut, and mahogany may be available at local lumberyards. The more fancy and rarer woods and veneers such as teak, rosewood, or other figured wood may have to be ordered through one of the specialty lumber companies that advertise in craft magazines.

Softwood such as pine and poplar or fir plywood may be used for the basic construction in a veneered project. These woods are more reasonably priced than hardwoods and are more readily available. The veneer is glued to the surface of the woods to complete the project. The use of veneers gives us the advantage of using the choicest wood grains and colors and the opportunity to match the grain for unusual and beautiful effects. The logs chosen for veneers are those with the best color and wood grain. Also, some of the rarer woods are only cut for veneers. The ability to match wood grains depends upon obtaining veneers cut successively from the same log (flitch). Since most projects require wood of ½-inch or ¾-inch thickness the change in the grain pattern would be too great to match. When the log is cut into thin sheets $1/28$ inch thick (the usual thickness of veneers), the changes in pattern between successive sheets is so subtle that one cannot notice them when matching the veneers.

Power and hand tools are used in the construction. With some skill and patience most of the projects shown could be sawed with a handsaw and miter box, but a small 7-inch table saw can cut almost all of these projects faster and more accurately than sawing by hand.

The following is a list of basic hand tools needed for all the projects shown:

Jack plane	Wood chisels
Block plane	Brace and bits
Hammer	Veneer saw
Various size nail sets	Utility knife
Try square	Steel straightedge or
Screwdrivers	yardstick
Hand drill with bits	Sanding block
Half-round wood file	Coping saw

The following is a list of power tools which can make construction easier and more accurate:

Table saw	Orbital or vibrating sander
Power jigsaw or	Disk sander or sanding disk
saber saw	for table saw
Electric drill and	
attachments or drill press	

The following are needed for holding wood while glue sets:

Bar clamps or pipe clamps for clamping long pieces
C-clamps
Band clamps
Spring type clamps
Rolling pin or photographer's roller for gluing veneer

Supplies needed for finishing include:

Sanding block of hardwood approximately ¾ inch by 3 inches by
    4½ inches or a commercial sandpaper holder
Aluminum oxide or garnet paper # 60, # 80, # 120, # 240, # 280
0000 steel wool
Cloth
Various finishing materials

A good variety of hand tools is necessary for all craftwork. If power tools are available, the need for some hand tools is lessened but not eliminated. A power saw with a planer blade will saw an edge smooth enough and accurate enough for gluing, eliminating the need for planing. A small plane is needed to help joint the edges of veneer for accurate matching. A half-round file is necessary to smooth curves cut with a coping saw or jigsaw.

An accurate straightedge, veneer saw and utility knife are about all you will need for cutting and matching veneers. The try square or larger framing square may be necessary for squaring edges of smaller and larger sheets respectively. Masking tape or gummed packaging tape is used for joining the matched edges of veneer before gluing. For finishing, various grits of abrasive paper on a flat wood block are needed. Fine steel wool is used to rub finishes to their final luster.

3

Basic Construction

The construction of most of the projects may be accomplished with a simple butt joint assembled with glue and nails. This joint would suffice as the surfaces could be veneered to hide the joint and the nail heads. If a joint is to be made with glue alone, a rabbet joint or rabbet and groove would be stronger.

If a joint is to be made with solid hardwood, a miter joint would conceal the end grain of the wood. If increased strength is needed, a spline may be added to the joint.

Projects formed with panels framed in solid wood, such as serving trays, require grooves in the solid edging and a tongue on the panel edge for strength. The grooves should never be deeper than half the thickness of the wood, otherwise loss of strength and splitting may result.

Most of the following plans are shown with butt joints, but any shown above could be substituted by altering the length of each piece to accommodate the particular joint.

The joints may be assembled by gluing and clamping the parts or by nailing.

C-clamps may be used to hold small glue joints while they dry. For larger joints bar or pipe clamps are needed. Band clamps are necessary for irregularly shaped projects, while spring clamps can be used to glue small pieces.

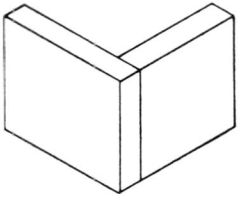

Butt

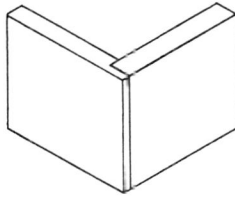

Rabbet

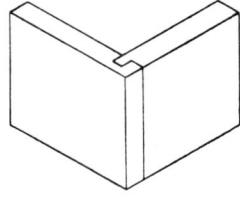

Rabbet & groove

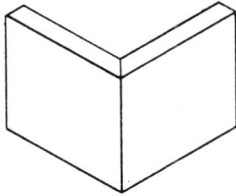

Miter

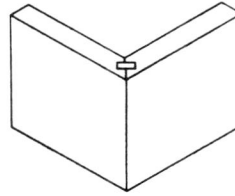

Splined miter

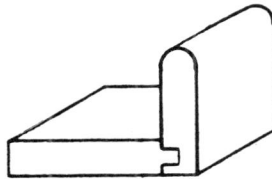

Tongue and groove

When fastening with nails use a nail with a length at least twice the thickness of the wood. For small projects driving the nail straight into the wood will suffice. For larger pieces toenailing (driving two nails close to each other at an angle toward each other) is stronger.

There are many glues available for use with wood. The polyvinyl or white glue is one with which we are all familiar. It comes in ready-to-use form and makes excellent joints for large and small projects. The aliphatic resins are similar to the polyvinyls, but stronger. Where a stronger joint is needed on larger projects, the urea resin or aliphatic resins should be used. For a waterproof joint the resorcin resins, a two-part powder and catalyst, work best. Epoxy cement is used where great strength is needed in a joint. It may not adhere to some woods which have a high oil content such as rosewood or teak. Contact cements are used today for gluing veneers, because

21

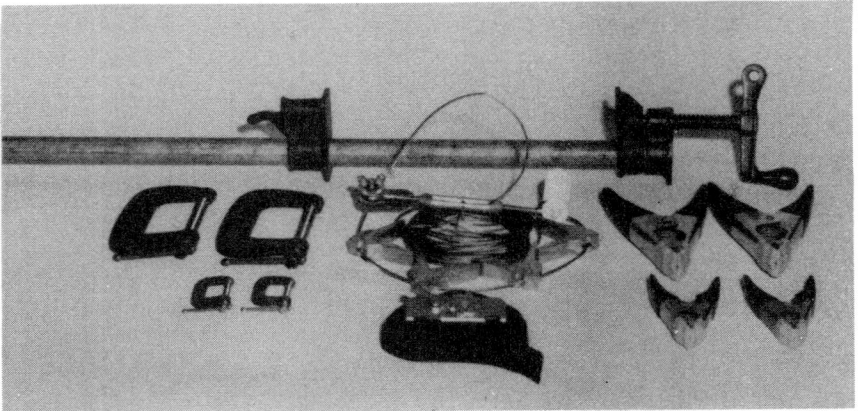

Clamps

of the ease of handling. When gluing veneers with a water-soluble glue, veneer must be glued to both sides of a panel, or there will be warpage, and large veneer presses must be available for all but the smallest projects.

4
Working with Veneers

Veneers are thin sheets of wood usually $1/28$ inch thick, but sometimes thicker or thinner, which are glued to other woods to form a panel. The most common use of veneers is in the formation of plywood.

Because of the thinness of the sheets of veneers, there is little change in the grain pattern between sheets. If veneers are purchased cut from the same flitch (log), they will be shipped as pieces cut successively and will match when glued successively into a panel.

Veneers are cut with a veneer saw or utility knife using a straightedge as a guide. A steel yardstick or framing square is easiest used. A try square used along the edge of the workbench with plywood or hardboard under the veneer works well with small pieces. The veneer saw seems to make the cleanest cuts with the grain, while the utility knife works best cutting across the grain.

When cutting veneers do not attempt to cut through the entire thickness in one cut. If shallow cuts are made, cutting each cut successively deeper until the wood is cut through, a more accurate joint will result. If the knife or saw is held at right angles to the veneer, little or no jointing may be needed for matching the joint. In cutting with the grain, position the straightedge so the grain of the wood runs toward the edge against which you will guide the veneer saw. Cutting this way will prevent the saw from following the grain away from the guide.

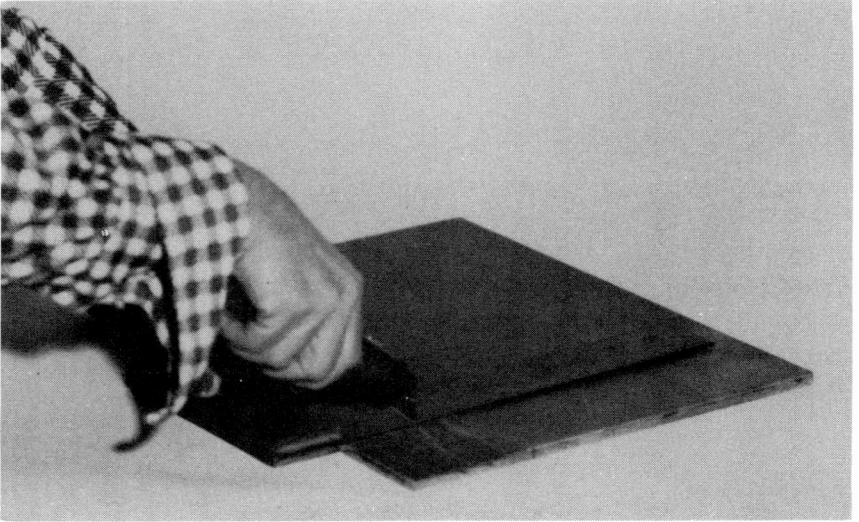

Cutting veneer across the grain

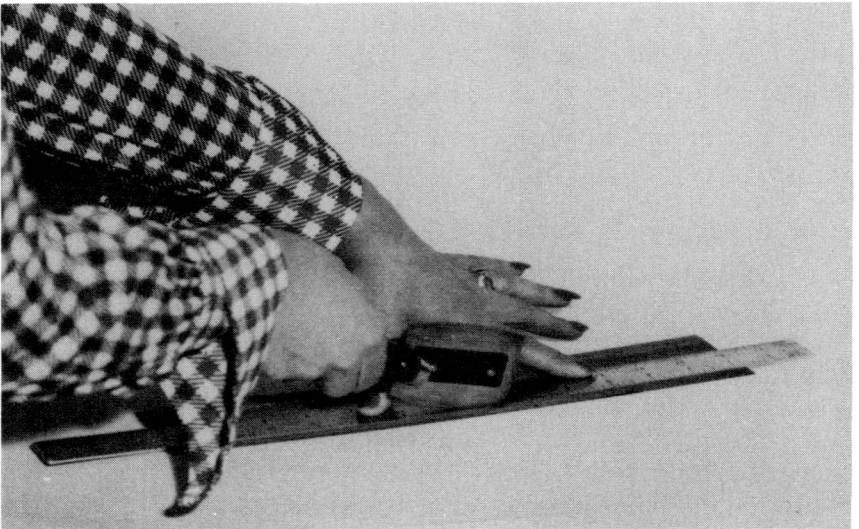

Cutting veneer with the grain

When the edges of the cut veneer are brought together for matching you will notice that the joint has spaces. The high spots where the edges touch must be removed. This is called jointing. Jointing may be done by planing the high spots with a block plane. If this proves difficult to do freehand, clamp the pieces of veneer

24

Jointing veneer

Taping veneer

between two narrower pieces of hardwood with perfectly straight edges. With the two edges to be matched projecting slightly from the hardwood, lightly plane the veneer, taking very fine shavings so the veneer edges meet the hardwood clamp.

After the pieces are cut and jointed, they are taped together. Heavy brown package sealing tape or veneer tape ¾ inch to 1 inch wide is

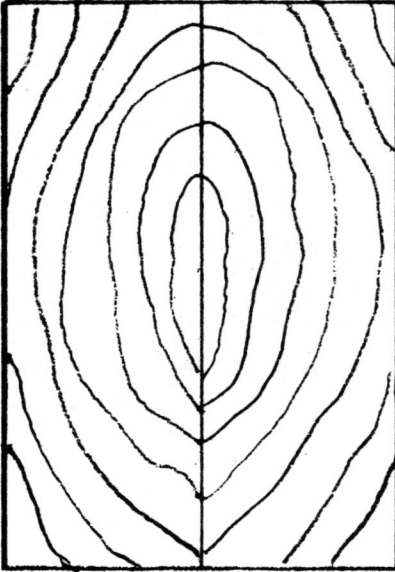

Book-matched

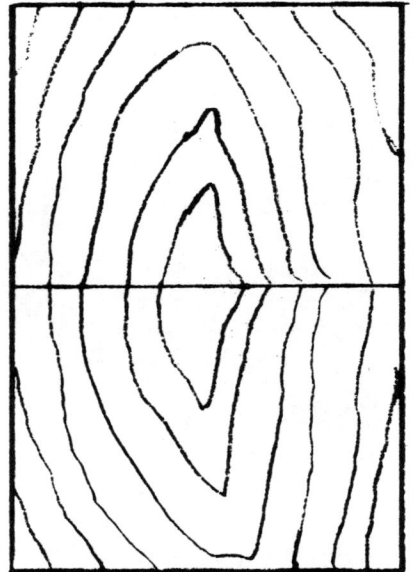

End-to-end match

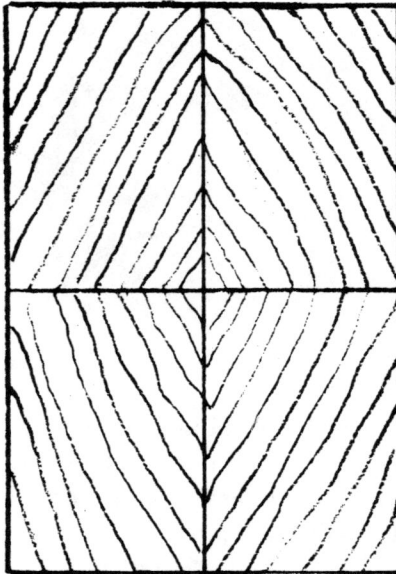

Diamond match
Drawings by author

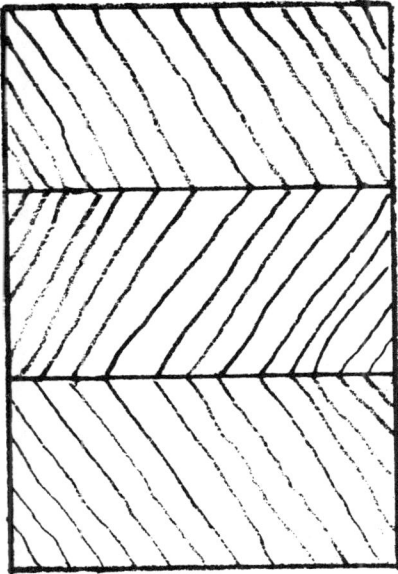

Herringbone

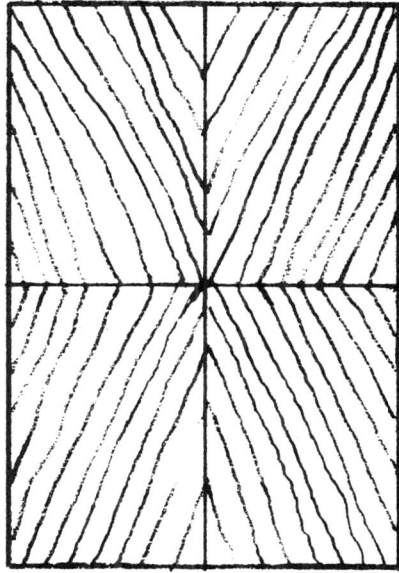

Reverse diamond match
Drawings by author

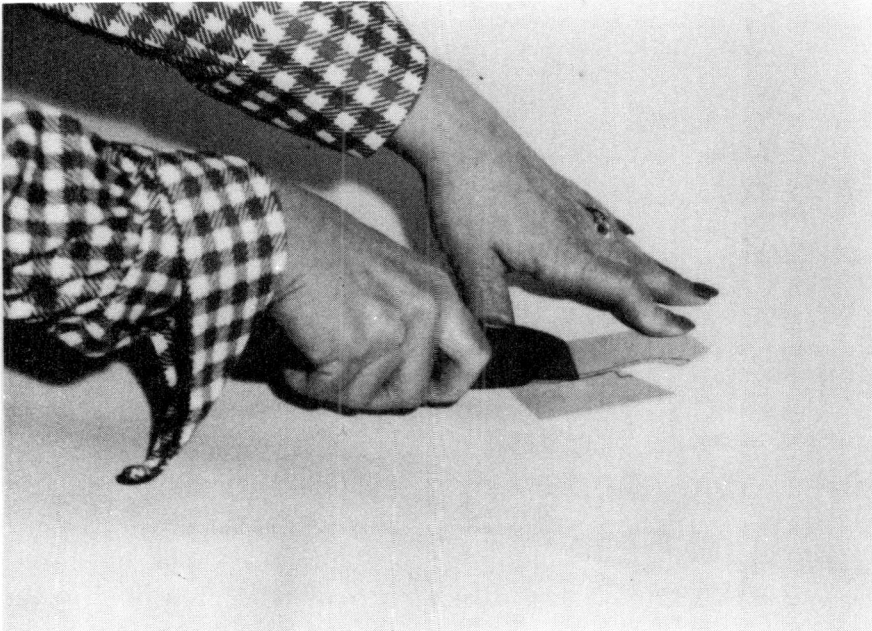

Cutting inlay monogram

27

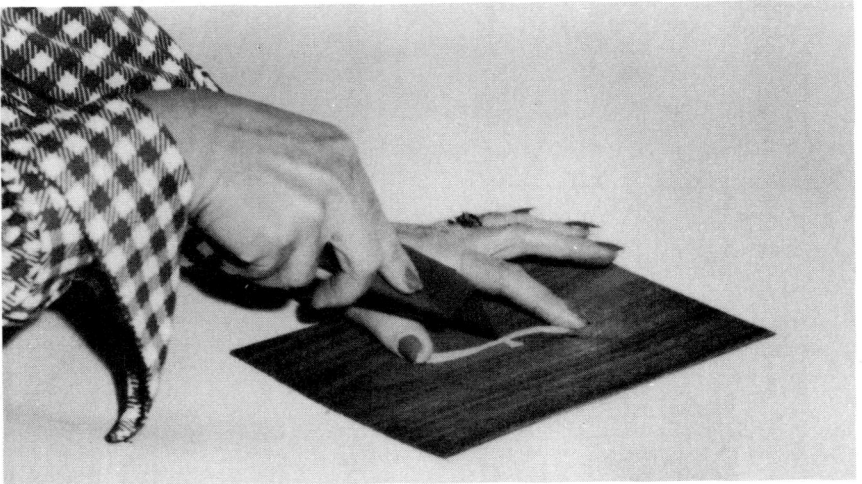

Scoring face veneer

Inserting monogram into face veneer

used. Avoid tapes with pressure-sensitive adhesives, as they lift the grain and splinter some woods. One piece of veneer must be flipped over and reversed in order for the grain to match. While holding the edges of the veneer in alignment, short pieces of tape are used across the joint to pull it together. Rub the tape vigorously with a finger until

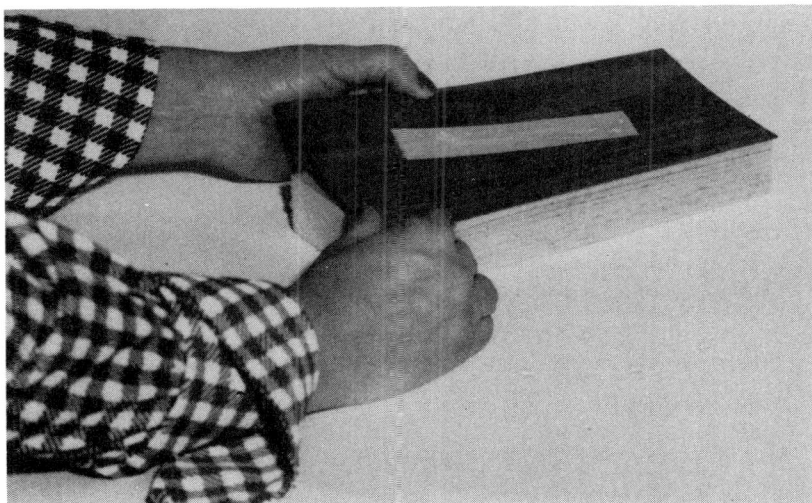

Gluing veneer

the adhesive dries or it will not stick well. A piece of tape the length of the joint is used to seal the entire joint.

Panels of veneer may be matched to give special effects. Flat-cut veneers may be side- or book-matched by matching lengthwise, turning over every other sheet as shown below, or irregularly matched in the order the sheets were cut from the flitch.

Panels may be matched end to end for the effect shown below. Panels such as the above could be book-matched to give further interesting effects. Striped or quarters-sawed veneer may be matched in the diamond-matched pattern shown below.

The grain may be matched parallel to the edges of the panel or at an angle as shown.

Two variations of the diamond match are a reverse diamond match and herringbone.

Other effects may be made by matching figured veneers such as crotches, butts, and burls. The matches shown above may be used simultaneously as shown in some of the projects in subsequent chapters.

One of the most beautiful uses of veneer is inlaying. Inlays are pieces of veneer that fit into recesses cut in the background veneer or solid wood. They may be purchased in various sizes, shapes, and colors or may be made from contrasting veneers. Inlays are rarely used in modern design, but monograms and the combination of materials other than wood are the exception.

When making an inlaid monogram choose a letter style which does not have parts too thin to cut from the thin veneer without breaking. Enlarge the design to the desired size and trace on the wood to be the inlay. Cut out with a utility knife making light cuts, each successively deeper, until the veneer is cut through.

Locate the veneer monogram over the area of the veneer panel to be inlaid. With a sharp knife lightly score around the outline of the monogram with the point of the knife exactly in the angle formed by the panel and the letter.

Remove the monogram and cut out the recess in the veneer. Hold the knife at right angles to the veneer to ensure an accurate fit.

Fit the two pieces of veneer together and securely tape into place.

Veneers may be glued using casein or urea resin glue, clamped between wood cauls or in a veneer press. When veneering in this manner, a backing veneer must be glued to the panel or it will warp. By using contact cement balanced construction is not needed as warping does not occur.

There are some contact cements formulated especially for gluing wood, but any of the major brands will work. Avoid unheard of brands as some are too thin to work well with wood. Coat both surfaces to be joined with the cement. When dry (usually one-half hour) coat again and let dry. When joining, the pieces must be exactly aligned, because when the glued surfaces meet instant adhesion occurs and the parts cannot be moved. To avoid air bubbles underneath, align one edge and hold the glued veneer at an acute angle to the work making sure the ends of the piece veneered will be covered. Slowly lower the veneer to the wood smoothing it into place with a flat rolling pin or photographic print roller. After the veneer is down tap the whole area with a rubber mallet or a hammer and block of softwood to make sure all areas are stuck down.

5
Finishing

Modern design calls for finishes which show the natural colors of the wood and its texture as well. No attempt should be made to fill open-grained woods.

Most veneers are sliced and have smooth surfaces, so little rough sanding is necessary. Medium (#120) garnet paper for hand sanding or aluminum oxide for power sanding will remove most marks found on the wood. This is followed by a sanding with #240 abrasive paper. Lightly wet the sanded surface with a small amount of water on a sponge and let dry to raise grain fibers and finish sanding with #280 paper.

A few sawed veneers have deep saw marks which must be removed before the above-mentioned finish sanding. Hand scraping and coarse sanding with #60 and #80 abrasive paper is needed first.

After sanding, vacuum or dust the sanded project. Use a tack rag to remove any fine dust that still remains before finishing.

Most projects are best finished with boiled linseed oil. The wood surface has a dull to slight sheen with open pores on open grained wood with the color slightly darkened. Use boiled linseed oil only, as it contains driers and hardeners. Raw linseed oil will not dry. Mix the oil with an equal amount of turpentine for the first application. Apply the oil generously with a clean brush or cloth (lint free). Allow the oil to soak into the wood for about 10–15 minutes, then wipe dry with a clean cloth and allow to dry for a day. A second application is made with undiluted boiled linseed oil which is allowed to again soak and is wiped off and allowed to dry. The finish is maintained by monthly applications of oil as general dusting is done.

Wax finishes (Minwax) are useful where a gloss finish is desired with little change in wood color. Staining may occur if chemicals spill, so use with care in places where beverage spills are likely to occur. The wax is applied with a soft cloth and allowed to dry (follow directions for the product). The surface is buffed vigorously with a clean, dry, soft cloth.

Where resistance to water, alcohol, and other spills is needed, the penetrating finishes may be used. These finishes penetrate the wood and combine chemically at the surface when they dry. Waterproof and alcohol-proof varnishes and lacquers are available in satin, semigloss, and gloss finishes. These finishes are applied with a brush, allowed to dry thoroughly (preferably overnight), sanded, and re-coated. Sand between coats with #240 or #280 abrasive paper. Two or three coats should give a chemical-resistant surface. After the last coat rub with 4/0 steel wool to flatten any irregularities in the surface of the finish and wax with paste wax.

PART II

Projects

1 Inlaid Monogrammed Bookends

The above design satisfied the need for custom-personalized bookends and is the end result of a design, which was originally a rectangular block of wood veneered on all sides.

Since compound miters are needed on the edging, a table saw or radial arm saw is best used for these cuts. Lacking these tools the joints may be sawed on a power jigsaw or saber saw with a very fine blade and the table tilted. A wood block and sandpaper can true up the joint.

Wood blocks 1 inch thick are cut 4 inches by 5¾ inches, beveling two sides and one end 12°. If 1-inch wood is unavailable, glue and nail ½-inch plywood keeping the nails well away from the areas where saw cuts will be made.

Cut two pieces of veneer for the faces and backs about ¼ inch larger than their respective surfaces. Form the monogram inlay veneered face as outlined in chapter 4. Thoroughly seal the inlay to the face veneer covering all of the monogram with veneer tape. Glue the veneer to the face of the block with contact cement making sure the monogram is centered. Trim the excess veneer flush with a knife or veneer saw at the same angle as the sides and ends are cut. Veneer the back of the block in a similar manner.

The thin band under the ¼-inch-solid border is a strip of veneer glued to one side of the border stock. Glue the strip to the ¼-inch-by-1¼-inch hardwood before mitering and gluing the edges.

Inlaid monogrammed bookends

When cutting to length, miter and bevel the top joints and miter the bottom. Glue the sides first making sure the strips are clamped with the inner edges of the miters exactly matching the corners of the block. A small brad at each end will prevent the strips from shifting. Clamp in a vise or with clamps using beveled gluing blocks while the glue dries. Plane the edging flush with the front and back, glue the ends, and trim. Round the edges on the face only with a block plane and sandpaper.

The base is $1/16$-inch galvanized sheet steel. Cut to the dimensions shown, smooth all edges with a metal file, and round two corners of each. Drill and countersink for small flathead wood screws. Countersink enough to allow the screw heads to be flush. Prime and paint the top (side opposite the countersinking) and edges. Flat black is the usual paint used for this purpose.

Chisel or rout a recess in the bottom $1/16$ inch deep, ¾ inch wide from the back of the block of the base. Center the recess between the ends. Screw the metal to the wood with ¾-inch flathead wood screws.

An oiled finish was used on the teak and maple. Thin felt is glued to the bottom and trimmed.

BILL OF MATERIALS

Number of Pieces	Size	Description
2	1″ × 4″ × 5¾″	Softwood
	Approximately 1 sq. ft.	Hardwood veneer
	Small Piece	Contrasting veneer
2	¼″ × 1¼″ × 24″	Hardwood trim
2	$1/16$″ × 4″ × 5″	Galvanized steel
	Felt for base	
6	¾″ #4 flathead wood screws	

34

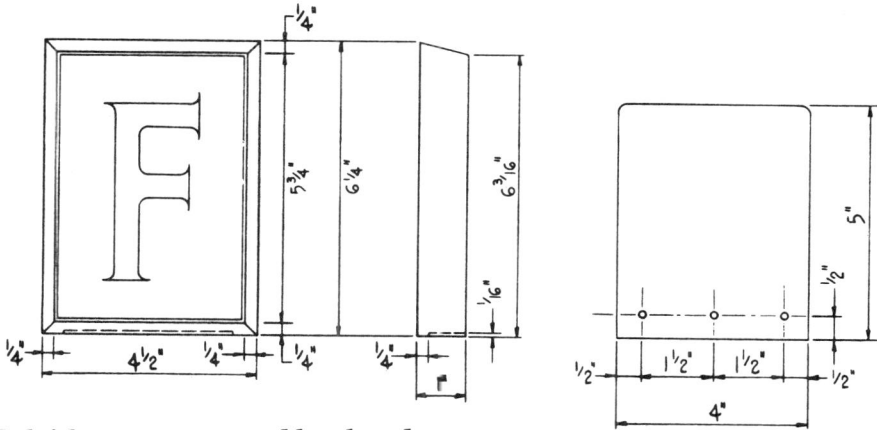

Inlaid monogrammed bookends

2　Large Monogrammed Serving Tray

Another personalized project is this large serving tray of Brazilian rosewood with a monogram of avodire. As shown the tray is strong enough for carrying filled glassware. If a stronger tray is desired, substitute ⅜-inch wood for the handles and edging allowing ¼-inch additional length to accommodate the increased thickness.

The face veneer and back veneer must be matched from two pieces to make the width shown. Choose the veneer with the best color and woodgrain for the face. A monogram of contrasting wood is inlaid in the face veneer in the position shown or centered if desired.

Cut ¼-inch fir plywood and carefully glue the veneer with contact cement and trim the veneer flush with the plywood. Rabbet the

Large monogrammed serving tray

bottom of the panel ⅛ inch from each edge deep enough to leave ⅛-inch-thick stock projecting to fit into grooves in the handles and edging.

Cut two pieces of ¼-inch stock approximately ⅝ inch wide for the tray edge. Enlarge the half pattern of the handle on heavy paper using a ½-inch grid. Transfer the handle shape to the wood leaving ¹/₁₆-inch to ⅛-inch additional stock at the bottom and ½-inch extra at each end for trimming and miters. Flip the pattern over to pencil the opposite side of the pattern. Saw the handles to shape with a fine blade on a jigsaw, saber saw, or coping saw. Drill holes of the proper diameter at the ends of the handle cutouts to facilitate sawing. Rout

BILL OF MATERIALS

Number of Pieces	Size	Description
1	¼″× 13¼″×20¼″	Fir plywood
1	¼″× 6″×24″	Hardwood
	4 sq. ft.	Hardwood veneer
	Small piece	Veneer for inlay

Large monogrammed serving tray

⅛-inch-wide grooves ⅛ inch deep, ¼ inch from the top edge of the straight edging and at the same level on the inside face of the handles. Round the top edges of the edging and handles and the inside of the handle cutouts using a block plane, file, and sandpaper. Thoroughly sand the top of the tray and the inside surfaces of the hardwood before assembly. Miter the ends of the handles to a length that the corners of the widest part of the plywood meet the bevel of the miter with the handhold exactly centered. Take great care using many small cuts if necessary to accomplish this. Align the handles and glue with waterproof glue using bar clamps for pressure. When the glue has set, miter the straight edging and glue.

When the glue has hardened, carefully chip away all excess. Lay the tray on a corner of the workbench upside down (not on the handles) and plane the excess wood flush with the veneered bottom.

Sand the remaining parts of the tray thoroughly including any glue left near joints on top. If voids are present in any joints, use the dust left from sanding mixed with white glue or airplane glue to fill.

Sand and finish with a waterproof and alcohol-proof finish. Sand between coats and rub the final coat with 4/0 steel wool for a dull rubbed finish and to flatten irregularities in the finish. Wax, if desired, with paste wax.

3 Laminated Bud Vase

The design for this project was inspired by the large amount of wood scrap one acquires in a few months of building other projects. The woods used were of varying thickness and color and were arranged for maximum contrast.

Cut the proper number of blocks 3 inches square of the woods listed or any other contrasting woods. Avoid laminating woods of similar color adjacent to each other for best effect. Glue all but the three bottom blocks making sure all surfaces are fairly even before clamping with a bar or pipe clamp. Polyvinyl or aliphatic resin glue may be used.

Drill a 1½-inch-diameter hole through the center of all the glued blocks. Glue and clamp the remaining blocks to the bottom.

The arc forming each side is made with a compass opened to 3 inches, the width of the block. With the point of the compass at the center of one side, an arc is drawn across the opposite side. Draw arcs for all four sides at each end of the block. Connect the ends of the arcs along the faces with the ends of the arc opposite for two opposite sides.

Laminated bud vase

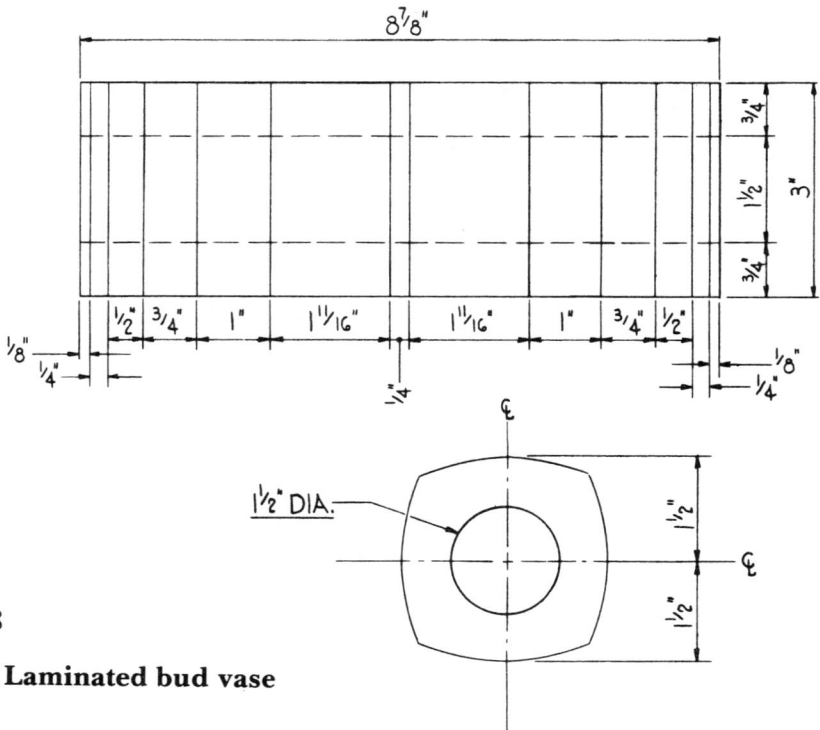

8⅞"

3/4"

1/2"

3"

3/4"

1/2"   3/4"   1"   1¹¹/₁₆"   1¹¹/₁₆"   1"   3/4"   1/2"

1/8"
1/4"

1/4"

1/8"
1/4"

₵

1½" DIA.

1/2"

₵

1/2"

Laminated bud vase

Remove the wood to the line forming the arc drawn on the ends with a wood rasp, medium and fine wood files, and sandpaper. The finish shaping is done with #80 coarse garnet or aluminum-oxide paper hand held. The opposite face is shaped and then the two remaining faces.

Sand thoroughly and finish with the finish of your choice.

4 Man's Jewelry Box

This jewelry box was designed as a twin for the woman's jewelry box that follows. Both are Brazilian rosewood veneer with Gaboon ebony edging on the bottom and top. For more contrast one of the lighter woods may be used. For variations in design the sides could be cut into a cove or V-shape and veneered. Three-quarter-inch wood must be used for these variations.

Start the box by cutting the ½-inch sides and ends from softwood or plywood. Glue and nail to form the box or substitute one of the joints shown in the first section. Dimensions shown are for butt joints, so they must be altered when using other joints. Cut the top and bottom from ½-inch stock.

Cut the veneer for the sides from a single 3-inch strip. If the sides are cut in sequence from the length, the grain will match on three corners. Save the most beautiful part of the veneer for the top. Veneer the sides of the box trimming the excess from each side before the next is veneered. Veneer both surfaces of the top, but do not

Man's jewelry box

veneer the bottom. Cut strips to veneer the top and bottom edges of the box mitering 45° at the corners. Glue the strips and trim flush with the veneered surfaces and the inner face of the box.

Cut the ⅛-inch hardwood for the top and bottom slightly wider than the edges, miter the corners, and glue opposite edges into place. Trim the excess flush. Fit, glue, and trim the remaining edges. Sand the bottom edges of the box and the edge of the bottom before assembly. Glue and brads are used for fastening. The top is hinged as shown with two ½-inch-by-¾-inch brass butt hinges. Mortises are cut into the inside surface of the top and the back edge of the box. Recess part of the hinge pin also, or the back edge of the top will be raised off of the edge quite a bit. Make sure the corner where the veneer does not match is in the back.

Sand all surfaces and finish with boiled linseed oil. Glue felt to the bottom and trim.

The inside of the box is lined with red velvet which is glued with white glue. Use the glue sparingly, or it will soak through the fabric. The bottom is lined with one piece and the sides with one strip cut oversize. Use a dull knife to push the material tightly into corners. A sharp knife will trim the excess at the end corner, and a sharp knife or scissors will trim the excess at the top edge after the glue has dried. One-quarter-inch-by-one inch strips covered with velvet on two faces and one edge are glued to the sides and bottom around the periphery inside the box. Three strips of polyurethane foam approximately ⅜ inch by ¾ inch are covered on two faces and one edge with velvet and glued on the bottom only to the rear of the box. This area is for cuff-link storage. A 1-inch covered wood strip is glued next in front

BILL OF MATERIALS

Number of Pieces	Size	Description
2	½″× 1½″×10″	Front and back
2	½″× 1½″×5″	Ends
2	½″× 5¼″×9¼″	Top and bottom
2	¼″× 1″×9″	Inside peripheral trim
2	¼″× 1″×4½″	Inside peripheral trim
1	¼″× 1″×8½″	Divider
1	¼″× ¾″×2¾″	Short divider
1	¼″× ½″×6⅜″	Divider
4	3/16″× ½″×2¾″	Dividers
	3 sq. ft.	Hardwood veneer
1	⅛″× 4″×13″	Hardwood trim

Small pieces polyurethane foam
One-half-yard velvet
Two ½″ × ¾″ brass butt hinges
Felt for bottom

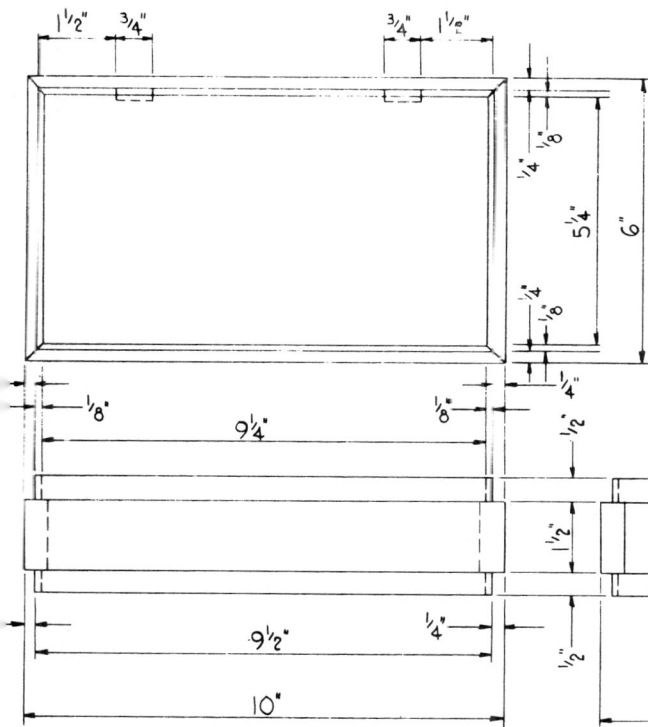

NOTE:
DIM'S ARE TYP. OF ALL CORNERS,
TOP & BOTTOM.

SEE NOTE

Exterior dimensions   **Man's jewelry box**

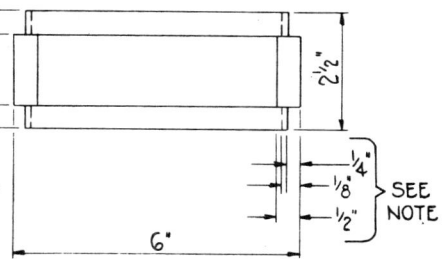

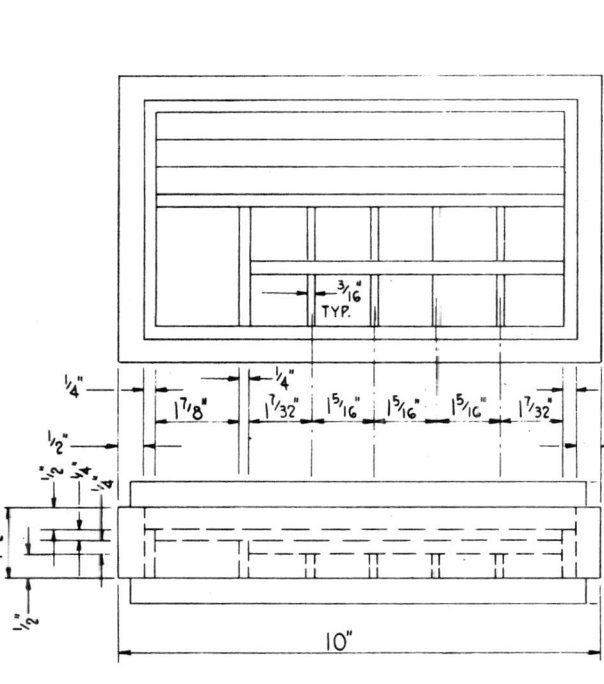

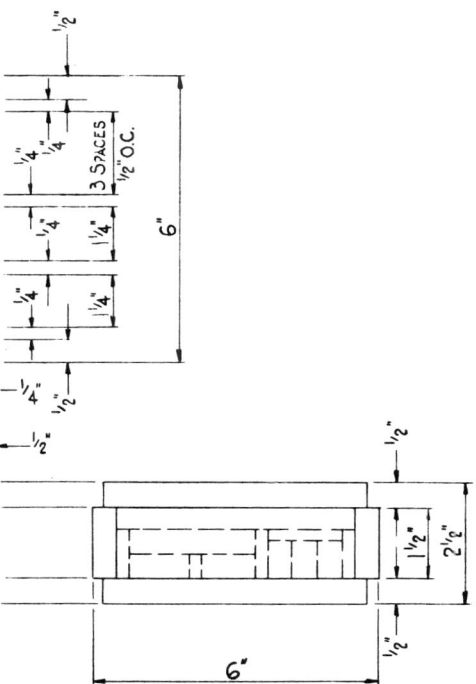

3/16" TYP.

3 SPACES
1/2" O.C.

Interior dimensions   **Man's jewelry box**

41

of the foam strips. Trim all covered wood for a snug fit. The large compartment on the left is made by gluing a ¼-inch-by-½-inch covered strip between the front of the box and the divider. The small compartments are made by half lapping ³/₁₆-inch-by-½-inch short strips of wood to a ¼-inch-by-½-inch long strip after covering with cloth. The half laps may be cut on a table saw after covering if a plytooth blade is used. Make all joints carefully so that they fit snugly. Also glue sparingly to avoid soaking the material. Glue the lapped wood on the bottom and only slightly in other places, and the jewelry box is finished.

5 Woman's Jewelry Box

This jewelry box is identical to the man's except for height. The increased height allows for two lift-out trays and a lower level, which are divided to accommodate various pieces of jewelry.

Cut and assemble the sides from ½-inch wood cut to the dimensions shown. Cut the top and bottom from ½-inch wood allowing ¼ inch each dimension for the hardwood trim. Glue and nail the joints to form the box or substitute one of the all-glued joints shown in the first section changing the length of the pieces to accommodate them.

Cut the veneer slightly wider than the sides and veneer successive sides from one length to match the grain on three corners. Trim the excess veneer from each side before veneering the next. Veneer both surfaces of the top reserving the choicest veneer for the top of this piece. Cut strips wider than the edges of the sides and veneer the top and bottom mitering the corners 45°. Glue the strips to the edges using contact cement taking care to align the miters. Trim the excess

Woman's jewelry box

veneer flush with the veneered surfaces and the inner surfaces.

Trim the excess veneer from the edges of the top. Cut the ⅛-inch hardwood edging slightly wider than the thickness of the top and bottom. Cut to length, mitering the ends, and glue opposite edges. Trim excess, glue the other edges and trim.

Sand the veneered bottom edge of the box and the edge of the bottom before assembly. Glue and nail to place using wire brads.

The top is hinged as shown with two ½-inch by-¾-inch butt hinges. Mortises are cut into the underside of the top and into the veneered back edge. Recess part of the hinge pin also. Make sure the corner where the veneer does not match is at the rear of the box.

Sand all surfaces and finish with boiled linseed oil finish. Attach the lid.

Construct two trays ¼ inch shorter and narrower than the inside of the box to allow for the fabric lining. The depth should also be ⅛ inch shorter than one third the depth of the box. Measure dimensions from the box, as they may vary slightly from the plans. The sides are ¼-inch-by-1-inch material with ⅛-inch plywood or hardboard bottoms butt joined and assembled with glue and brads. The dividers are ¼ inch by 1 inch and should be long enough to fit snugly after the inside of the tray is lined.

Line the bottom of the box with a piece of velvet. The sides are lined with one piece of cloth cut oversize. Using a small amount of white glue spread over the wood surface being glued, press to place eliminating air bubbles or creases. Work the cloth into the corners with a dull knife. Cut any excess material at the last corner with a sharp knife. When the glue is dry trim the top edge with a sharp knife or scissors. Cut the ¼-inch-by-1-inch peripheral edging and dividers. Cover the peripheral wood on two faces and one edge, cut to fit snugly, and glue to the sides of the box. Cut the dividers to divide the bottom as shown on the plan. Cut the grooves for the half laps about $1/_{16}$-inch oversize to allow for the added thickness of the cloth. Cover both faces and the top edges. After trimming excess cloth and cutting so all pieces fit snugly, glue the lapped joints, and glue to the box on the bottom only. The top edges of the dividers can be fastened with ½-inch #19 or 20 gauge brads driven at an angle into the peripheral wood. Countersink the heads below the velvet and the hole will hardly be noticeable.

Measure the inside, height, thickness of the inside and outside and then cut a piece of velvet to cover the tray with one piece of fabric. On the back of the cloth lay out a pattern of all the surfaces covered in two dimensions. Cut the waste out of the four corners leaving extra on the usable piece to allow for error. Glue the area marked for the bottom

BILL OF MATERIALS

Number of Pieces	Size	Description
2	½"× 3½"×10"	Front and back
2	½"× 3½"×5"	Ends
2	½"× 5¼"×9¼"	Top and bottom
2	¼"× 1"×9"	Inside peripheral trim
2	¼"× 1"×5"	Inside peripheral trim
1	¼"× 1"×8½"	Bottom long divider
3	¼"× 1"×4½"	Bottom short divider
4	¼"× 1"×8¾"	Long tray sides
4	¼"× 1"×4¼"	Short tray sides
2	¼"× 1"×8¾"	Long tray dividers
3	¼"× 1"×2¼"	Short middle tray dividers
2	¼"× 1"×4"	Short upper tray dividers
2	⅛"× 4⅞"×8⅞"	Tray bottoms
	3 sq. ft.	Hardwood veneer
1	⅛"× 4"×13"	Hardwood trim

One yard velvet
Two ½" × ¾" brass butt hinges
Felt for bottom

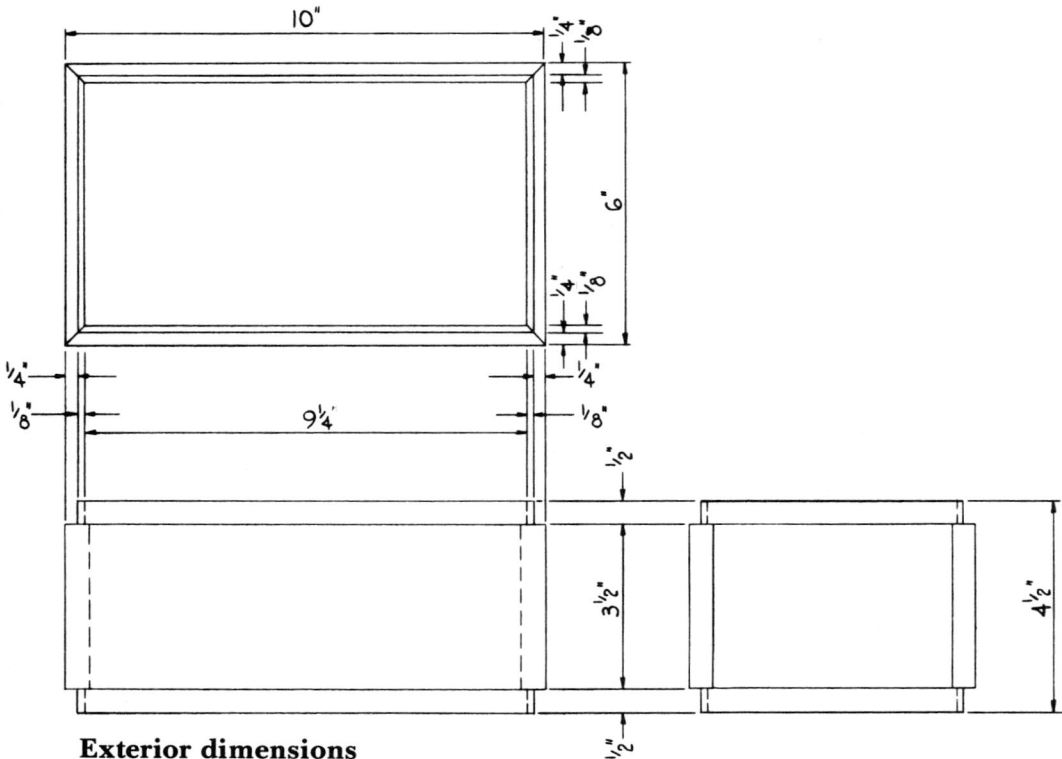

Exterior dimensions

Woman's jewelry box

BOTTOM MIDDLE TOP ¼" DIVIDERS, TYP. TOP, MIDDLE, & BTM. TRAYS

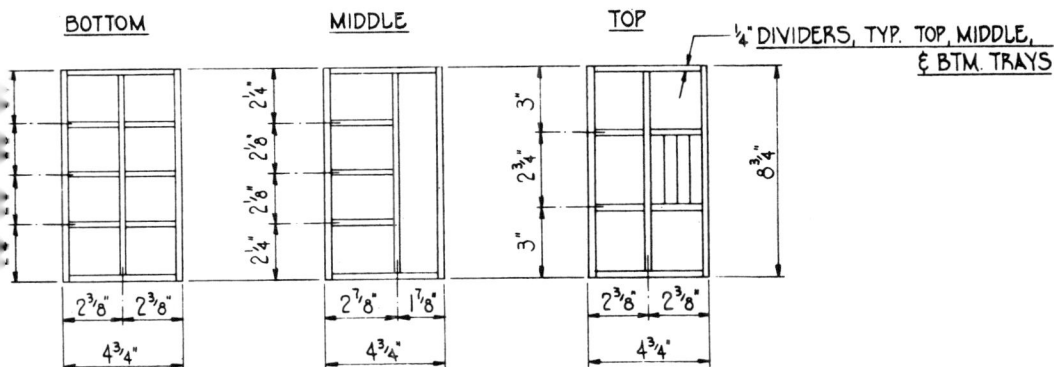

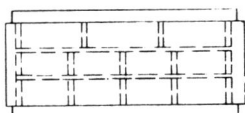

Interior dimensions   Woman's jewelry box

inside to the bottom of the tray. Use a putty knife or dull table knife to push the fabric into the corners. Glue the vertical walls to the inside of the tray cutting excess material from the corners with a sharp knife. Do not cut any excess material which will go over the top edge or the corners will not be covered. When gluing the top edge cut the material at 45° to miter the corner. Glue material from three sides over the outer surfaces of these sides and trim flush with the bottom and corners when the glue is dry. The long piece left will cover the outside of the remaining side and is folded to cover the bottom. Trim the edges flush when dry.

Cut and cover the dividers for the tray as shown in the plan and complete as was done for the bottom. The top tray has four pieces of cloth-covered foam (⅜ inch by ½ inch) covered with cloth on three sides and glued in one compartment to hold rings.

Glue felt to the bottom and trim when the glue is dry.

6 Desk Set

This project is six matching pieces made in zebra with ebony trim. The blotter pad is of generous size for an executive-size desk but can

Desk set

be made any size to fit any desk. Select Gaboon ebony is difficult to obtain, so another wood such as walnut may be substituted.

a   Blotter Pad

The ends are made from two ½-inch-by-2-inches-by-20-inches zebra with ½-inch-by-½-inch-by-20-inches Gaboon ebony glued to one edge. Align the top face of the wood carefully, so minimal finishing will be necessary.

With a router form a recess ⅛ inch deep by 1½ inches wide in the underside in the zebra. Leave ⅛ inch of wood at the ends. Square the corners of the recess with a knife and chisel.

The pad section is made of ⅛-inch acrylic plastic glued into the

Blotter pad

Number of Pieces	Size	Description
2	½" × 2" × 20"	Zebra
2	½" × ½" × 20"	Gaboon ebony
1	⅛" × 19¾" × 32"	Acrylic plastic
	8" × 20"	Felt

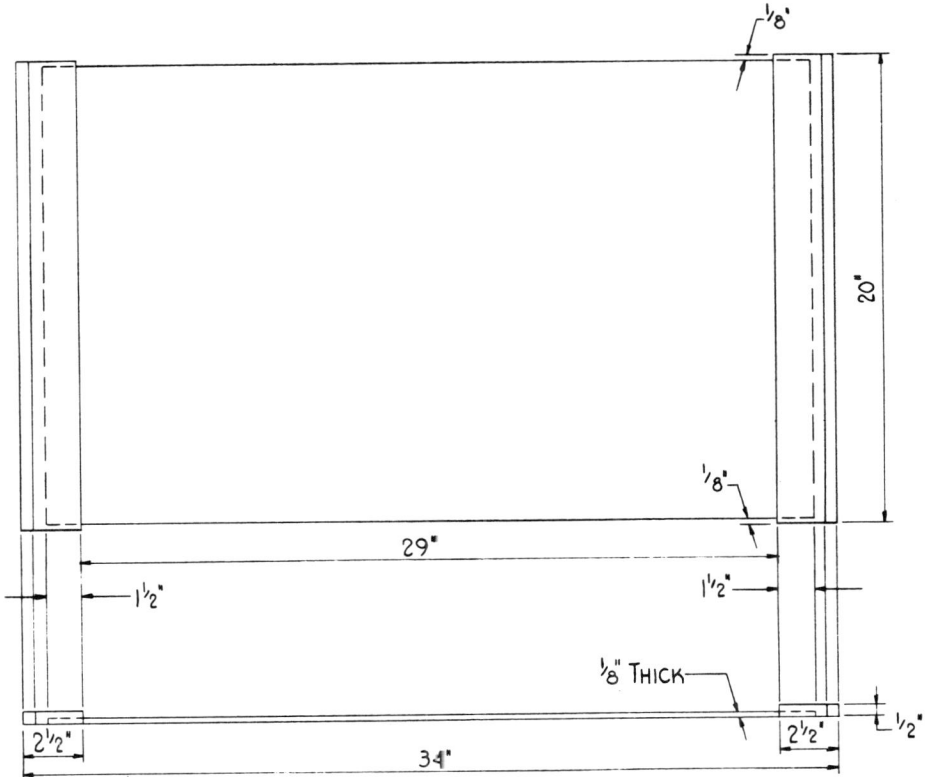

Blotter pad

recess. Consult your plastics dealer for the special cement required.

Thoroughly sand and finish the wood with a boiled linseed oil finish before assembly. Glue felt to the ends under the wood.

b Pencil Holder

Start by drilling a 1½-inch-diameter hole in a 1¾-inch square block of zebra 4 inches long. If a drill press is not available drill a larger size

Pencil holder

BILL OF MATERIALS

Number of Pieces	Size	Description
1	1¾"× 1¾"×4"	Zebra
1	1¾"× 1¾"×1"	Gaboon ebony

block (longer also for squaring the ends) and plane and sand to size centering the hole. Square the ends. Carefully glue a 1¾-inch-square, 1-inch-thick piece of Gaboon ebony to the bottom of the zebra. If 1-inch ebony is unavailable, glue from two ½-inch pieces.

Sand all surfaces flat and smooth. Finish with boiled linseed oil finish.

Cover the bottom with a piece of felt.

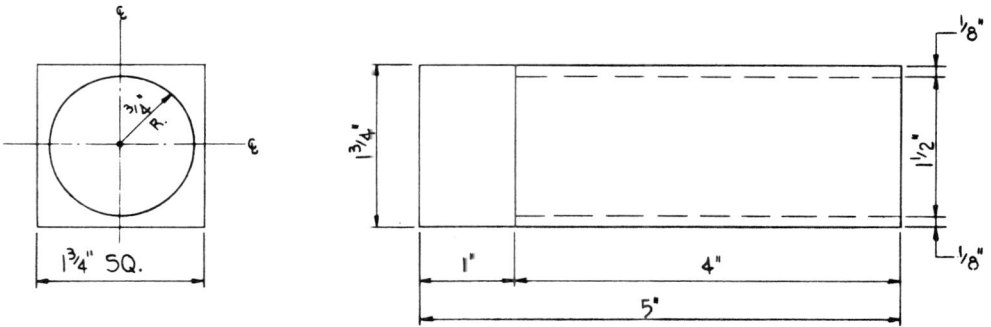

Pencil holder

c Letter Opener

The blade of the letter opener is made from a flat all-metal letter opener available in most stationery stores.

Cut the handle as shown by the dotted lines in the plan to form a tang to glue into the wood handle.

The handle is made of two pieces of ⅛-inch zebra and one piece of ⅛-inch Gaboon ebony shaped as shown. Cut slightly oversize to allow for final shaping. Cut a piece out of the ebony to allow the tang of the metal blade to fit into the handle.

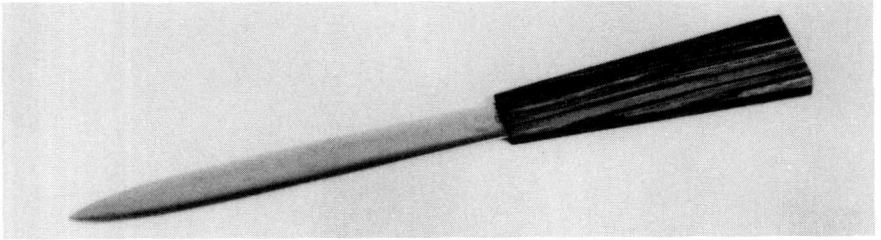

Letter opener

BILL OF MATERIALS

Number of Pieces	Size	Description
2	$\frac{1}{8}'' \times 1\frac{1}{4}'' \times 4''$	Zebra
1	$\frac{1}{8}'' \times 1\frac{1}{4}'' \times 4''$	Ebony

Metal letter opener

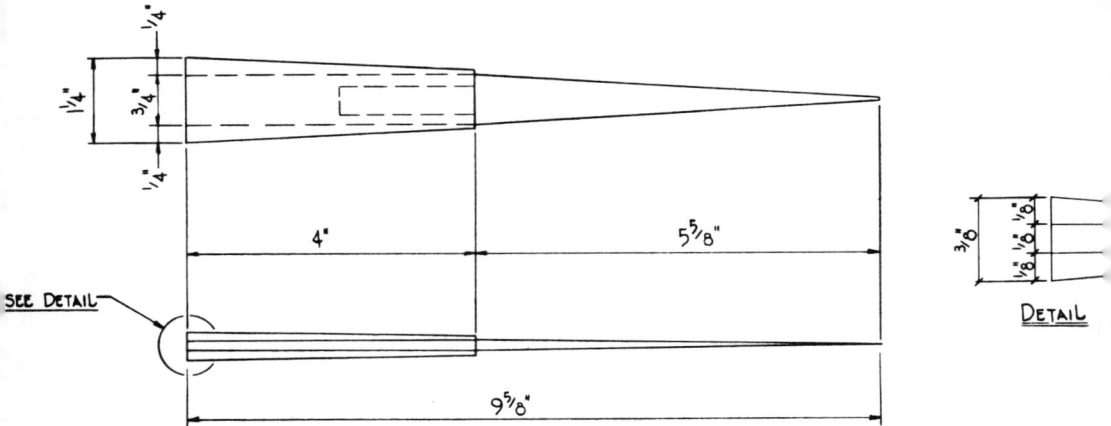

Letter opener

Glue the three pieces of wood with the blade inserted into the recess with epoxy cement.

Trim the edges even, slightly plane the faces to reduce the thickness near the blade, sand, and finish with boiled linseed oil.

d   Stamp or Paper Clip Box

The cover of the original box was made of ¼-inch zebra carefully mitered at the angles shown and glued together. If an accurate table

50

Stamp or paper clip box

saw is not part of your equipment, consider cutting the shapes from softwood and covering with veneer. Cut approximately $^1/_{16}$-inch undersize to allow for the veneer thickness.

To start the cover cut two strips of ¼-inch zebra 1 $^5/_{16}$ inch wide. Cut each piece of the form in succession, so the grain will match when glued together. Glue the pieces with a glue such as Duco, as these parts cannot be clamped. If an oily wood is used, wipe the end grain with lacquer thinner to remove oil from the surface of the cut which will allow a stronger joint. Cut ⅛-inch ebony for the sides and a piece for the middle strip matching the profile of the forms. Carefully glue the ebony to the two forms. The inside vertical pieces are made from ¼-inch wood or a wedge-shaped piece may be glued so that a space is not present at each end. This will also result in a stronger joint. If you

BILL OF MATERIALS

Number of Pieces	Size	Description
2	¼″ 1⁵⁄₁₆″×4⅝″	Bottom
3	⅛″× ¼″×4⅝″	Bottom
4	¼″× 1⁵⁄₁₆″×2⅜″	Top
4	¼″× 1⁵⁄₁₆″×1⅛″	Top
4	¼″× 1⁵⁄₁₆″×⅜″	Top
3	⅛″× 2¼″×5½″	Ends and divider
2	¼″× 1⅜″×2¾″	Verticals inside top
3	⅛″× 1⅛″×3⅜″	Sides and divider, base
2	⅛″× 1⅛″×2¾″	Ends, base
1	⅛″× 1⅛″×2½″	Divider, base

51

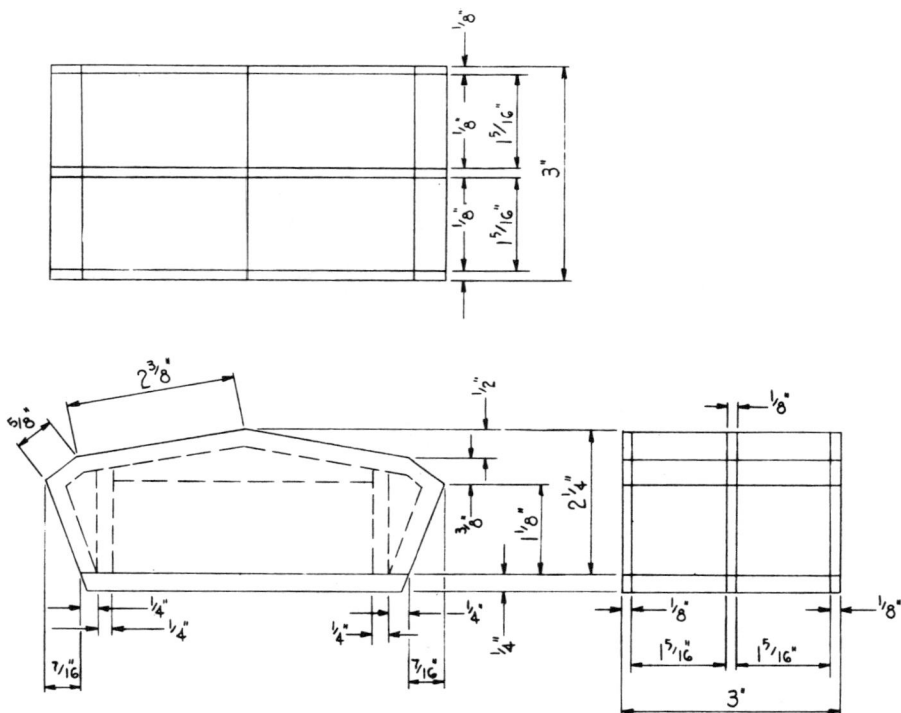

Exterior dimensions
Stamp or paper clip box

wish to finish the inside of the cover, glue the ebony sides after the forms and middle strips are glued and finished.

The bottom is constructed of strips of ¼-inch hardwood and ⅛-inch trim as was the top. Carefully finish the bevel with a disk sander or abrasive paper on a wood block.

The divided box which is glued to the base is made of ⅛-inch-by-1⅛-inch zebra. The short and long divider section are half lapped. Sand the inside surfaces of all pieces before assembly. After gluing the half-lapped joint, glue and clamp the sides and ends. Sand the outside of the assembly making sure it will slide into the cover without binding before gluing to the base.

When sanding the top use a sanding block to hold the abrasive paper. Sand carefully avoiding the rounding of any surfaces or corners. When sanding the surface that meets the beveled edge of the base clamp both parts and sand together.

Finish with boiled linseed oil.

52

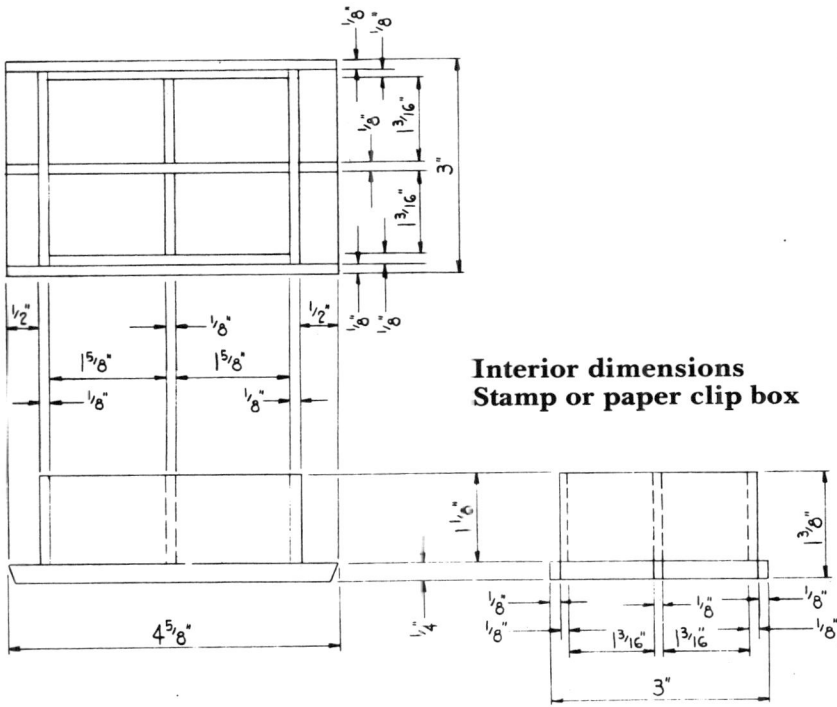

Interior dimensions
Stamp or paper clip box

e   Bookends

Prepare 1-inch blocks of softwood or glued plywood. Veneer two faces and the top with hardwood veneer. Cut a ¼-inch groove about ⅛-inch deep with a router or on the table saw in the center of one face and across the top.

Cut ¼-inch Gaboon ebony for the sides and strips for the grooves. Cut all pieces slightly oversize to allow for any gluing error and sand flush after assembly.

Rout the $^1/_{16}$-inch-deep recess for the metal base.

Thoroughly sand the wood and finish with a boiled linseed oil finish.

Cut the base from $^1/_{16}$-inch galvanized steel. File and sand the edges smooth with a metal file and emery cloth. Drill and counter-sink the holes for ¾-inch #4 flathead wood screws. Prime and paint the top (side opposite the countersinks) of the metal. Screw the metal into the

Bookends

BILL OF MATERIALS

Number of Pieces	Size	Description
2	1″× 3¾″×6¼″	Softwood or plywood
4	¼″× 1¹/₁₆″×6¼″	Ebony-ends
2	⅛″× ¼″×1″	Ebony
2	⅛″× ¼″×1″	Ebony
	1 sq. ft.	Zebra veneer
2	¹/₁₆″× 3¾″×5″	Galvanized steel
6	¾″ #4	Flathead wood screws

Felt for base

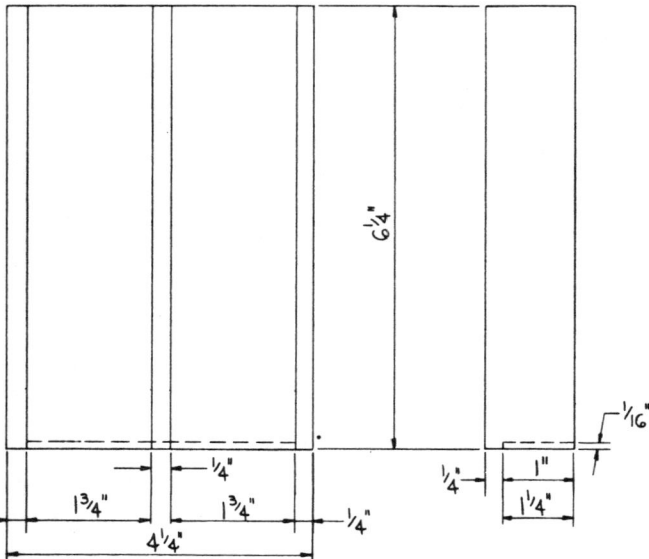

Bookends

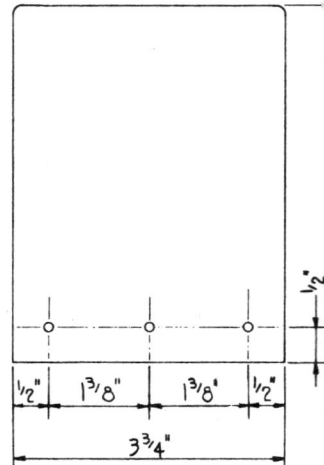

54

recess, glue felt to the bottom, and trim flush with the metal and wood.

f Calendar Holder

To simplify the cutting of grooves in wood this thin, the frame is made from two thicknesses of hardwoods glued together after making the saw cuts.

Cut $\frac{1}{8}$-inch-by-$\frac{1}{2}$-inch and $\frac{1}{4}$-inch-by-$\frac{5}{8}$-inch strips of hardwood about 30 inches long. Rabbet the $\frac{1}{4}$-inch strip $\frac{1}{8}$ inch wide by $\frac{3}{16}$ inches deep leaving a $\frac{1}{16}$-inch lip on the front face. Rabbet the $\frac{1}{8}$-inch strip $\frac{1}{8}$ inch wide by $\frac{1}{16}$ inch deep leaving a $\frac{1}{16}$-inch lip.

Miter the $\frac{1}{4}$-inch wood to form a frame for the front. Glue with epoxy. Cut the $\frac{1}{8}$-inch strip to form a three-sided frame for the back. Miter the top piece at both ends and the sides at the top only. The bottom of the side pieces are squared with the bottom of the frame. Glue the $\frac{1}{8}$-inch strips to the back of the $\frac{1}{4}$-inch frame to form a channel with two different depths, one for the calendar insert, the other for the back.

When the cement is dry, cut $\frac{1}{4}$ inch from the bottom and right side of the complete frame. Glue ebony to these sides to restore the original width.

Cut $\frac{1}{8}$-inch hardwood $\frac{1}{16}$ inch wider and $\frac{1}{8}$ inch longer than the dimensions of the rear opening. Rabbet $\frac{1}{16}$ inch by $\frac{1}{16}$ inch across the two ends and one length to form a lip which fits the groove in the

Calendar holder

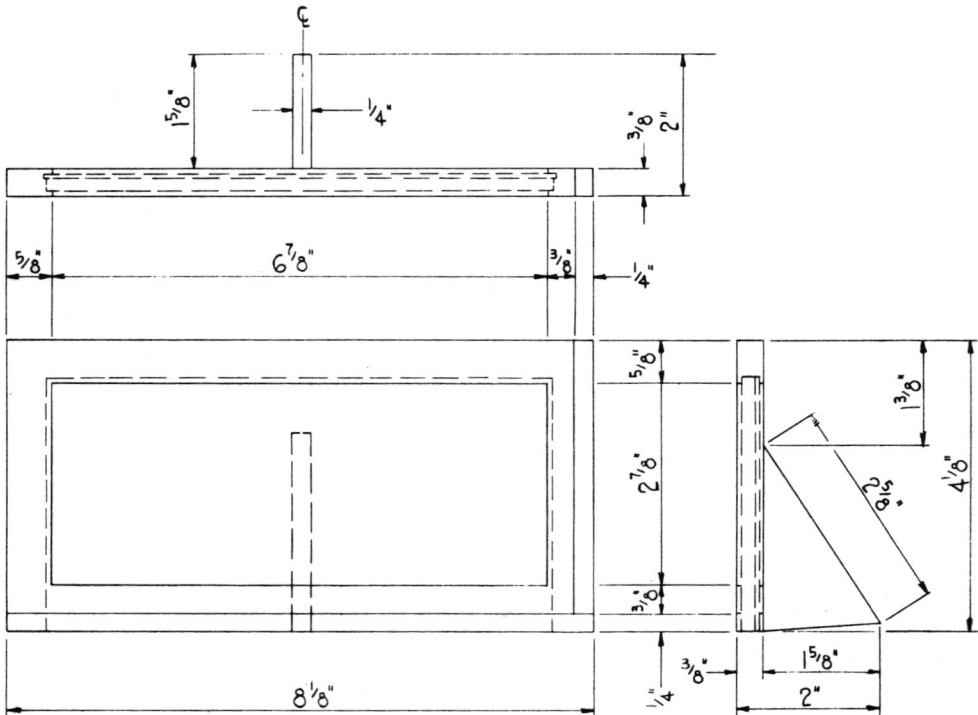

Calendar holder

BILL OF MATERIALS

Number of Pieces	Size		Description
2	¼″×	⅝″×8⅛″	Front frame
2	¼″×	⅝″×4″	Front frame
1	⅛″×	½″×8⅛″	Rear frame
2	⅛″×	½″×8″	Rear frame
1	⅛″×	3⁹/₁₆″×7″	Back
1		¼″	Hardwood standard
1	¼″×	⅜″×8⅛″	Ebony trim
1	¼″×	⅜″×4″	Ebony trim

frame. Cut the ¼-inch wedge standard and glue to place in the center of the back after sanding.

Thoroughly sand all wood parts for finishing. Adjust the back by sanding, so it slides easily in its groove.

Finish with boiled linseed oil.

This calendar holder was designed to use the National #55-925 calendar refill.

56

g Veneered Wastebasket

The basket is constructed by laminating posterboard and wood veneers to form a cylinder. A form must be built around which the posterboard and veneers are glued.

The form consists of two disks of ½-inch plywood sawed and sanded to 9¾-inches diameter. Connect the disks with four 1-inch-by-2-inch wood strips nailed equidistant at the edges of the disks. The disks support the ends of the materials, and the strips prevent caving in in the middle as the cylinder is glued.

The cylinder is made of two sheets of double-weight posterboard veneered inside and out with hardwood veneers. If you do not want to veneer the inside, substitute an additional thickness of posterboard for the inner veneer.

Veneered wastebasket

Trim a sheet of posterboard the height of the form. Wrap the sheet tightly around the form, mark, and cut the joint to butt. Put the sheet on the form with the joint over a wood strip and tape with masking tape. Short pieces across the joint may be necessary before taping the whole joint with one piece. Cut the second (and third sheet if being used) slightly wide to allow for any error in gluing. Cut the length so the edges butt when wrapped over the first. Mark a vertical line on the first sheet using the partially wrapped second sheet as a guide when gluing. Stagger all vertical joints for strength. Do not glue any joint on top of another one. Glue the second sheet to the first with contact cement. Trim any excess material from the ends. Glue the third sheet if the veneer is to be omitted from the inside.

Match the veneer for the outside, taping all joints securely. Locate and accurately trim the butt joint, glue the veneer over the poster-board, and trim excess.

Push the form out of the cylinder. Match veneers for the inside of the basket and trim the butt joint at the ends. Glue to place with contact cement rolling the veneer into a small cylinder and unrolling as it is glued. An extra pair of hands is useful for this operation.

Cut a ¼-inch plywood bottom for the cylinder or use one of the ½-inch ends of the form reducing the diameter to fit the veneered cylinder. Cover the inside surface of the disk with veneer if the inside of the basket is veneered.

Trim the bottom to fit tightly and glue into the bottom of the basket.

Cut the strips of ebony veneer for the trim. Sand off saw marks, if the veneer is sawed before assembly. Fit the bands around the outside, carefully mark and cut the lengths for a perfect joint, and glue to place using band clamps for pressure. Fit the ebony inside band for a very tight fit. The pressure formed at the butt joint will hold the band in place while the glue dries. The top edge may be veneered with mitered strips of veneer cut in arcs and glued to the

BILL OF MATERIALS

Number of Pieces	Size	Description
2	½"× 9¾" dia.	Plywood-form
4	1"× 2"×14"	Softwood-form
2 or 3	15" × 31"	Posterboard
1	¼"× 9¾" dia.	Plywood bottom
3	1/24"× 1"×31"	Ebony-trim
2	1/28"× 15½"×31"	Hardwood veneer

Pieces of ebony for top trim

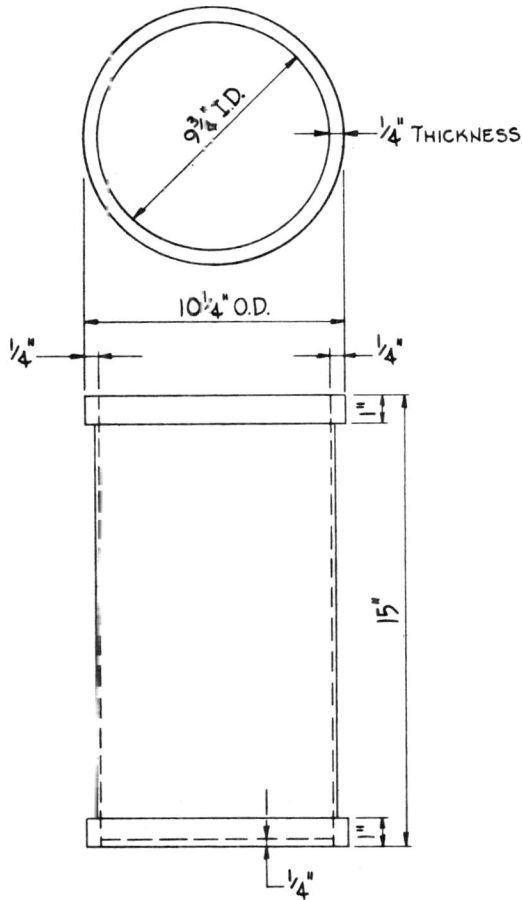

Veneered wastebasket

edge. Cut slightly oversize and sand flush with the trim already glued in place.

Sand well and finish with a boiled linseed oil finish.

7   Walnut and Tile Table Lamp

This lamp is walnut-veneered plywood with solid walnut trim forming a frame for random-sized ceramic tiles. The tiles used were white with grey and brown.

The sides are cut from ¾-inch plywood and butt jointed with white glue and nails. The rabbets at the top and bottom may be routed after

Walnut and tile table lamp

assembly. If a router is not available make a ¼-inch-deep saw cut ½ inch from the top end and 1½ inches from the bottom end. Chisel the rabbet across the width of the narrower sides. Leave ¾ inch of wood at either edge of the wider sides for gluing and nailing to the narrow pieces. Glue and nail the top and set aside the bottom until the lamp is assembled.

Veneer the sides and top. Trim the veneer flush.

The ¼-inch strips of walnut are glued into ¼-inch wide grooves routed ³/₁₆ inch deep. Chisel out the rounded corners of the groove before gluing and miter the ends of the walnut strips. If a router is unavailable glue and nail ¼-inch-by-³/₁₆-inch strips using 19 gauge or smaller brads ½ inch long.

Locate the center of the top and bottom and drill a ⅜-inch-

Number of Pieces	Size	Description
2	¾″× 4¾″× 19⅞″	Sides
2	¾″× 3¼″× 19⅞″	Sides
2	½″× 3¾″×3¾″	Top and bottom
	¼″× ⅜″×14′	Walnut strips
	4 sq. ft.	Walnut veneer
	15′	Lamp wire
	19⅝″ long	⅛″ Treaded pipe
2		Small wire nuts
2		Lamp sockets

Double cluster
Felt
Four d. finishing nails
Plug
Hex nut

diameter hole for the lamp parts. Drill a ³/₁₆-inch hole ½ inch from the bottom in one side for the lamp wire.

Soak the tile to remove the mesh backing. Before gluing arrange the tile in the center panel to determine approximately how many of each size tiles are needed to fill the space leaving approximately equally spaced grout lines. Mask the tops of the wood strips to avoid staining with cement and grout. Dry the tiles and cement larger tiles first using the smaller ones to fill in the remaining spaces. Leave at least ¹/₁₆-inch lines between tiles for grout. Allow the cement to harden, mix the grout according to the directions on the package, and push the paste deeply into all lines and recesses. Wipe the excess grout from the tile. When the grout is almost hard (note setting time from the package), polish with a soft cloth. Seal with silicone sealer after the grout has cured for a few days to prevent dirt from becoming embedded and discoloration.

The lamp is assembled with a double adjustable cluster. One-eighth inch threaded pipe ⅝ inches long is screwed into the bottom of the cluster and inserted into the top of the lamp. The bottom is inserted into the rabbet and the pipe into the hole. A round or hex nut is tightened to hold everything together.

If the tubing for lengthening the cluster is short, replace with longer tubing. Remove the cover from the top and thread one end of a length of lamp wire through the pipe into the cluster. Cut short lengths of wire, bare the ends, wire and attach each socket to the cluster threading the short wires into the cluster. Attach one wire from each socket to each wire brought up from the base. At the bottom tie a knot in the wire at a point where it will touch the wood inside the recess without exerting tension on the wire in the lamp.

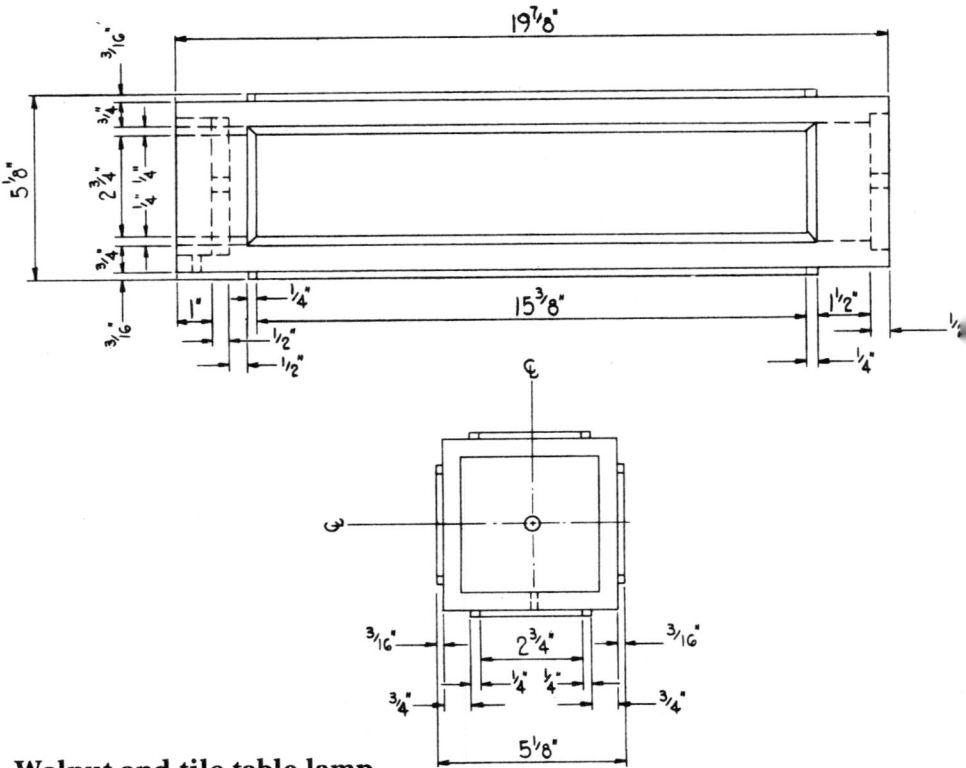

Walnut and tile table lamp

Push the rest of the wire through the $^3/_{16}$-inch hole and attach a plug to the end.

Glue felt to the bottom. A lamp shade approximately 15 inches in diameter and 18 inches long was used.

8 Hardwood Lamp

This lamp was made of hardwood scraps of varying thicknesses. The thicknesses shown or any sized blocks to give the length shown may be used.

The blocks are beveled 5° on the table saw. The large width of each

62

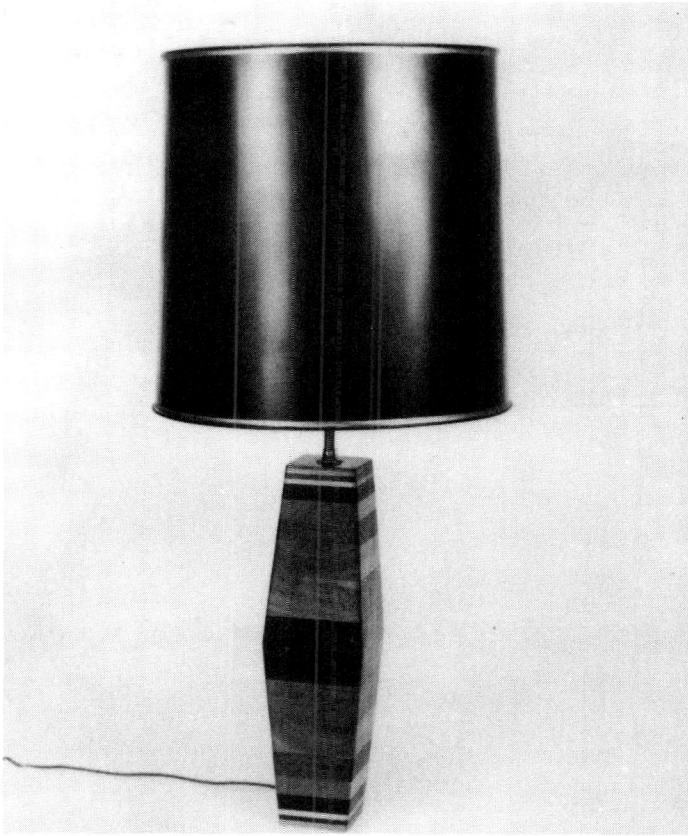

Hardwood lamp

block is cut the size of the smaller width of the previously cut larger block. The middle block is 4⅞ inches at the center beveled toward each face. The succeeding wood is cut from this starting point.

Locate the center of each block and drill a ⅜-inch-diameter hole on a drill press. Assemble the wood with glue on the ⅛-inch threaded pipe and clamp on opposite sides with bar clamps. Align the edges of adjoining blocks as accurately as possible and tighten the clamp screws.

Sand the surfaces flush with coarse or extracoarse abrasive paper. A belt sander can make this work easier and faster. Round the corners along the length to about a ¼-inch radius with a file and abrasive paper. Round the sharp edge at the center.

Counterbore the base 1 inch diameter, 1 inch deep. Drill a ³/₁₆-inch-diameter hole ¼ inch from the bottom in the center of one side into the counterbore for the lamp wire.

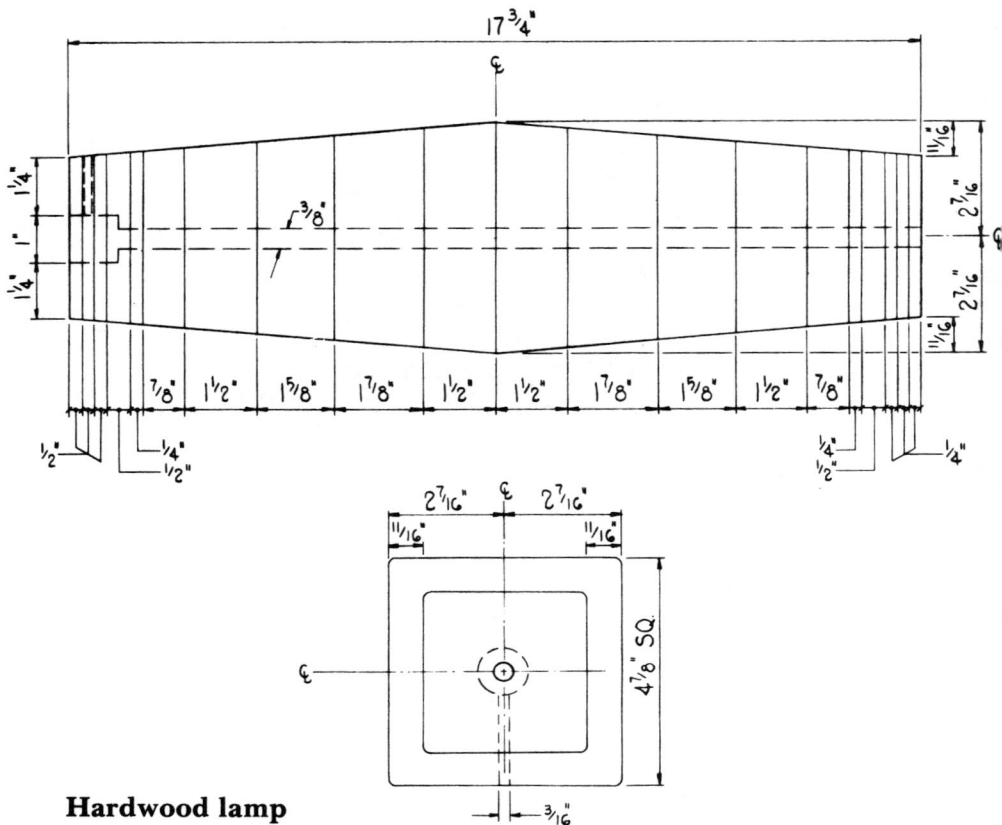

Hardwood lamp

BILL OF MATERIALS

Number of Pieces	Size	Description
	17½″	Threaded lamp pipe
	15′	Lamp wire
2		Wirenuts
2		Lamp sockets
1		Nut to fit pipe

Scrap hardwood of varying thicknesses ¼″ to 3″ between 3½″ and 5″ square
Double cluster
Plug.

Finish sanding with successively finer abrasive papers to 6/0. Finish with semigloss lacquer or penetrating resin finish without filling the open grain of any open grain woods.

Attach a double cluster to a 17½-inch length of ⅛-inch threaded pipe, insert into the base, and tighten a nut at the bottom. If the brass tubing for extending the cluster is very short, replace with a longer one. Wire the lamp sockets and attach, running the wires inside the cluster. Push one end of the remaining wire through the small hole into the counterbore hole, tie a knot where the wire enters the hole in the side and through the pipe into the cluster. Attach one wire from each light socket to one wire from the plug with wirenuts. Attach a plug to the other end of the wire.

Glue felt to the bottom of the lamp and trim.

This lamp takes a parchment shade (black in the original) about 16 inches in diameter and 18 inches long.

9   Powder Shelf

This shelf was designed to fit into a corner in a foyer. It could also be built straight with a square edge to fit along one wall in a corner or with two beveled ends to occupy the middle of a wall. The original was made of Gaboon ebony with a Macassar ebony border.

The shelf is made of ¾-inch plywood, butt-jointed with glue and dowels or with Tite-Joint fasteners to the dimensions shown or your own dimensions. A triangular piece of plywood is glued and clamped into place to form the angle in the corner. The end angles are cut $117°$ measured at the wall side or $27°$ measured from the front. The front edge and ends are built up with ⅜-inch-by-1-inch stock glued and nailed to the underside of the shelf. The corner is cut and filed to a radius of 1⅝ inches.

Gaboon ebony veneer is sawed $1/24$ inch and has deep saw marks on both surfaces. Carefully plane, scrape, and sand to remove the marks to get a flat surface for cementation. The opposite side may be finished after gluing.

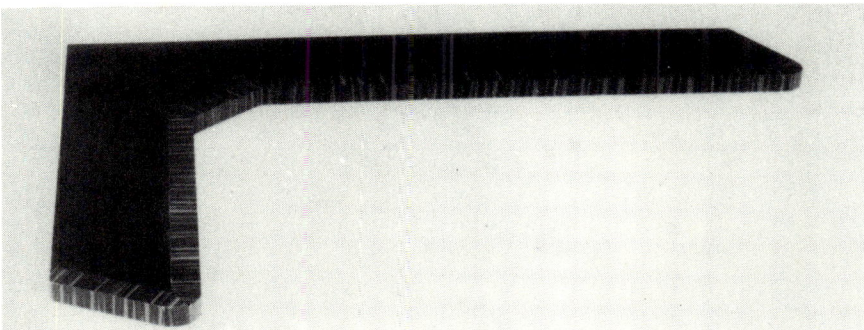

Powder shelf

To veneer this project the edges of the Gaboon ebony must meet the line where the Macassar edging begins. After laying out the lines on the shelf, match the width to 6½ inches, cut the end near the inside corner to 70° as shown in the plan, and the outer end to 27°. Be sure all veneer edges are jointed where other veneers will be matched. Glue the Gaboon to the long side first, cut and match the irregular corner piece jointing the three edges which will match with other veneers, and lastly glue the short side. If carefully done 1½ inches of wood on the edges will be unveneered. Carefully trim any excess due to faulty measuring.

Trim excess veneer from the back edge and remove saw marks taking care not to thin the veneer too much where the edging veneer will be cemented.

Cut Macassar ebony across the grain into 1⅛-inch strips for the edge and 1⅝ inches for the border. Joint the edges and match in lengths to be glued. If the strips for the border and edge are cut successively (1⅝-inch strip first, 1⅛-inch strip next) matching at the edge of the shelf will occur.

Glue the 1⅛-inch strips to the edges first with contact cement making sure the veneer covers the whole edge, as it has not been cut oversize. Carefully bend around the corners and trim the excess at the end.

Cut the miters and glue the short piece of border at the inside corner first. Cut the miter at the outside angles to meet at the center of the curve or trim wedge-shaped pieces to make the veneer grain appear to be bent around the curve. Finish the ends with a short straight piece. Carefully trim all excess with a sharp knife and file.

Remove the excess thickness of the Gaboon ebony with a cabinet scraper or by sanding until the thickness of the two types of veneers is the same. Finish sanding being careful to remove all sanding marks from the coarse sanding. Avoiding the use of the orbital sander with

BILL OF MATERIALS

Number of Pieces	Size	Description
1	¾″× 8″×35½″	Plywood
1	¾″× 8″×24″	Plywood
1	¾″ triangular piece	Plywood
1	1/24″× 6½″×38″	Gaboon ebony
1	1/24″× 6½″×28″	Gaboon ebony
1	1/24″ piece for corner	Gaboon ebony
	2 sq. ft.	Macassar ebony
1	⅜″× 1″×8′	Pine or plywood

Powder shelf

this hardwood will make finish sanding easier.

Finish with a boiled linseed oil finish.

Hang with decorative shelf brackets, one on each wall, screwed into a stud.

10 Mirror Frame

The mirror frame pictured matches the ebony shelf. The molding may be cut from a 1¼-inch turning square, but less waste is left if a 1¾-inch square is cut diagonally to yield two lengths. Certain striped woods such as zebra, if finely striped outside, may not show grain when cut diagonally.

Start by squaring 36-inch-and 14-inch long turning squares on a jointer or bench saw with a planer blade. Remove as little stock as possible. With the saw blade tilted 45° rip the pieces diagonally to form two lengths triangular in cross-section.

Mirror frame

The first cut is made with the saw blade at 90° to the table (0° on most saws). Remove stock from one corner making the wood 1¼ inches wide (see illustration).

For the second cut tilt the table 38° and position the fence to the left of the blade. With the surface formed by the last cut facing the blade adjust the fence so the next cut starts at the angle nearest the bevel. The wood should now have the proper bevel and a ½-inch-wide face adjacent to the bevel.

The third and fourth cuts form the groove for the mirror. One-eighth inch of wood should be left adjacent to the face bevel. Set the saw blade to 0° and adjust the fence to the right of the blade to make the first cut approximately ⅜ inch from the bottom of the stock. The blade should cut ¼ inch deep. With the ½-inch face on the saw table make the third cut. Adjust the fence to cut a ¼-inch-wide cut to the edge of the blade opposite the fence to finish the groove.

The fifth cut is made at 5° with the beveled face down. Remove only ⅛ inch of stock.

Number of Pieces	Size	Description
1	1¾" × 1¾" × 36"	Hardwood
1	1¾" × 1¾" × 18"	Hardwood

Mirror, cardboard, ½" #3 roundhead wood screws
Picture frame wire

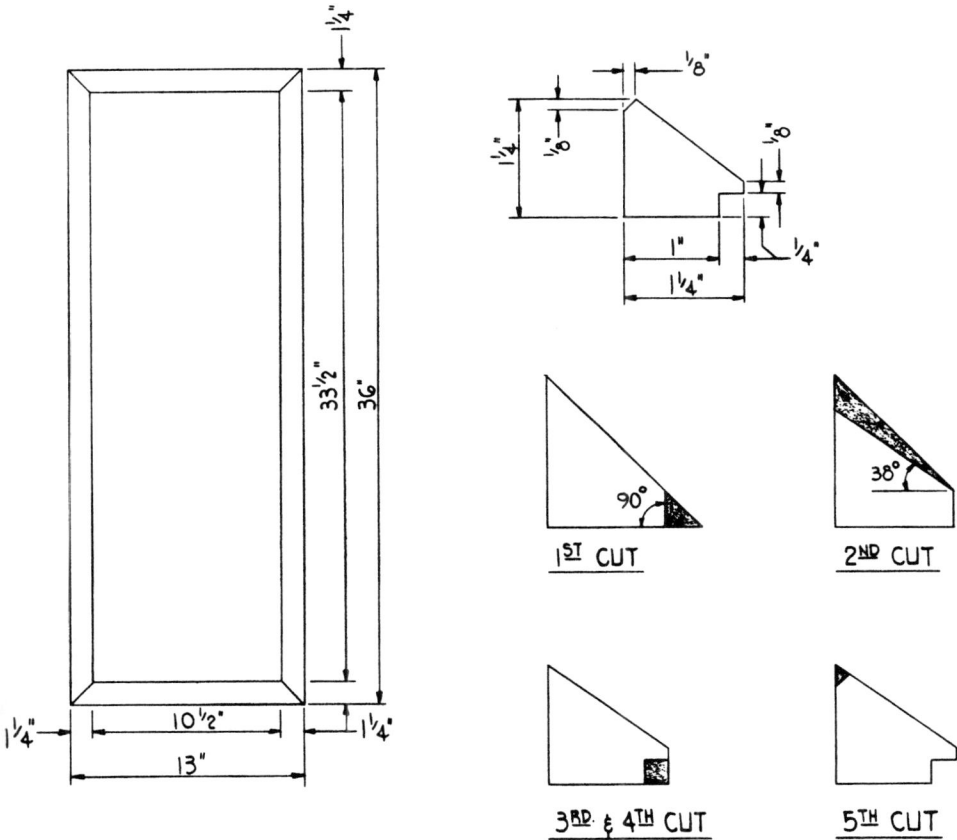

Mirror frame

If a hollow-ground blade was used, the cuts should be smooth enough to sand. If deeper marks are present use a cabinet scraper or coarse abrasive paper to remove the marks before finish sanding.

Miter the ends of the molding 45° cutting the wood to the proper length. Glue with epoxy cement clamping with corner clamps.

Finish with a boiled linseed oil finish.

One-eighth-inch sheet mirror is fitted into the back and is covered with heavy cardboard. Small brads or glazier's points are pushed into the side of the groove at the corners and three places on the long sides to hold the mirror in place.

Drill a $^1/_{16}$-inch hole ½ inch deep 12 inches from the top into the back of the frame to fasten picture frame wire. Make a small loop in the wire and attach with a ⅜-inch or ½-inch #3 roundhead wood screw in each hole. Leave a slight bow in the wire.

When hanging use two wall hooks a few inches apart to prevent the mirror from tipping.

11   Shelf Brackets

These hardwood brackets are used in various arrangements by nailing or screwing to wall studs. An alternate design may be had by substituting angles for the curve shown, as indicated by the dotted lines on the drawing.

The brackets are sawed with a saber or jigsaw. Irregularities are removed with a half-round file and abrasive paper to produce smooth flowing curves. A curved block of wood should be used to hold the paper to prevent the edges from becoming rounded.

Drill a $^3/_{16}$-inch or larger hole at a 45° angle in the upper corner for fastening the bracket to the wall. Counterbore the top so the head of a wood screw will be below the top surface when the bracket is fastened.

Drill a ¼-inch-diameter hole ¼ inch deep ½ inch from the outer bracket edge. Glue a ½-inch length of ¼-inch dowel. Chamfer the

Shelf brackets

Size of Squares	Bracket Size	Shelf Width
¼"	2⅝"	3½"
½"	5⅛"	6"
¾"	7¼"	8¼"
1"	10½"	12"

edges of the dowel with a small file, so it will enter the holes easier. Use the table below to make patterns for various sized brackets.

Shelves are made of solid hardwood or veneered plywood. More work is involved veneering the plywood, but there is less chance of warpage, especially in the wider shelves.

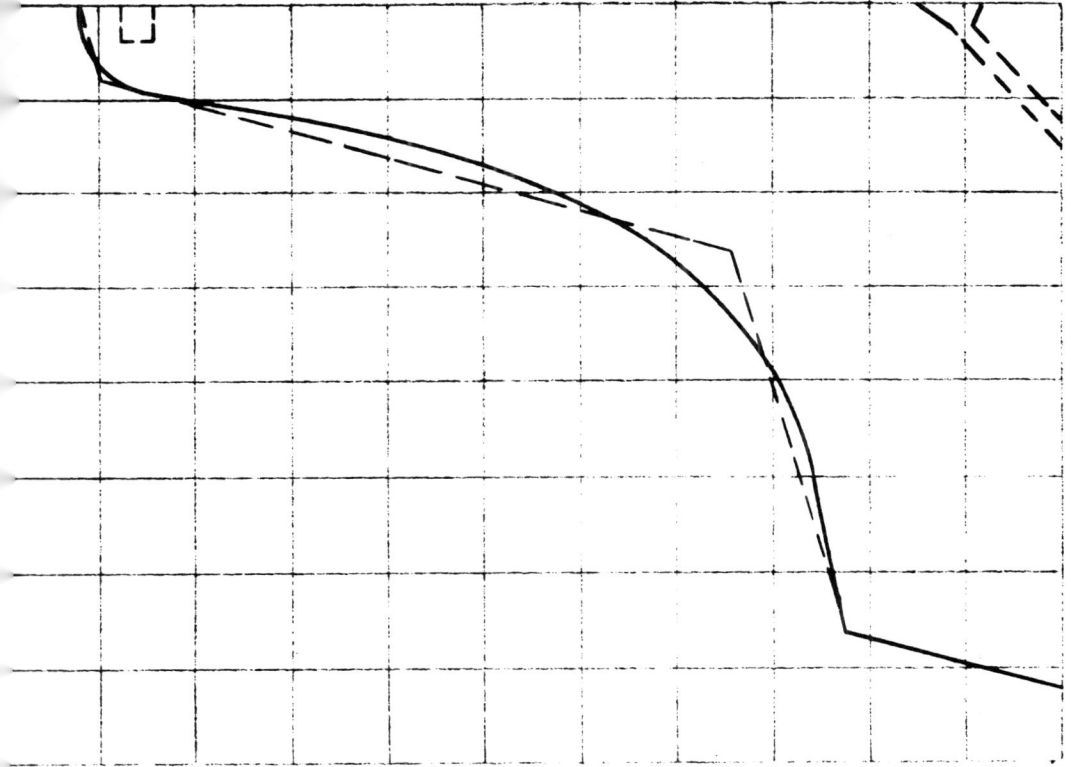

½" SQUARES

Shelf brackets

After cutting the shelves to size, prepare the veneer for the two faces slightly oversize. Veneer the front edge and ends with any waste and trim flush. Glue the face veneer and trim the excess.

Sand and finish the brackets and shelves.

Using a stud finder locate the beams in the wall. After finding one stud the others should be easy, as they are usually 16 inches on center. Insert a 3-inch flathead wood screw in the angled hole, hold the bracket over the stud at the proper height, and hammer the screw through the plasterboard of the wall into the stud. Screw tightly into the wall. Locate the position of the other bracket and level it with the first before screwing to the wall.

Carefully center the shelf on the brackets. Mark the position of the dowels on the underside of the shelf and drill ¼-inch holes. When installing force the dowels into the holes to keep the shelf in place.

12 Octagonal Planter

This planter was designed for use with artificial flowers. If a flower pot is to be used inside, make the planter higher to make it even with the top edge of the pot. The diameter as shown should accommodate a four-inch pot.

Octagonal planter

Number of Pieces	Size	Description
8	½"× 2"×4"	Teak staves
8	⅛"× ⅝"×4"	Maple
8	⅛"× 2"×4"	Hardboard scrap
1	½"× 4¾" octagon	Base

Veneer for edge of base

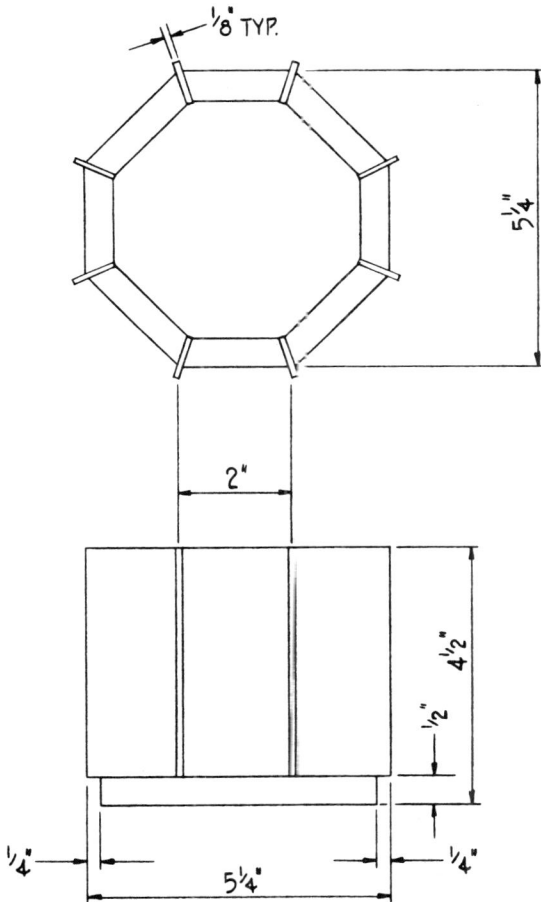

Octagonal planter

The planter pictured was constructed of teak and maple. The edges of the bottom were veneered with ebony but may be sanded and painted flat or semigloss black.

Construction is started by cutting the half-inch teak staves. Using a

73

hollow-ground blade on a table saw rip the stock 2 inches wide beveling the edges 22½°. One-eighth-inch-thick maple is cut ⅝ inch wide. Cut to length and sand thoroughly before assembly.

Since the maple strips protrude ⅛ inch from the sides, ⅛-inch scrap wood or hardboard is clamped with the sides to maintain even pressure. Shift any pieces which may have slipped out of alignment and allow the glue to harden.

Coat the beveled edges of the staves lightly with glue. Assemble on the workbench with the maple strips in place. Clamp with two band clamps placing one at the bottom first to hold the ⅛-inch scrap in place. Position the top clamp and tighten each gently for even firm pressure and allow the glue to harden.

Cut the octagonal base 4¾ inches as shown. If ebony veneer is to be used for the edge, the bottom must be made smaller, if the veneer is ¹/₂₄ inch thick. Veneer the edges or sand and paint black. Glue the base into place weighting while the glue dries.

If the maple strips do not protrude uniformly, plane and sand for a regular appearance. Remove any excess glue and finish with one coat of semigloss sealer and wax.

13 Small Serving Tray

The tray, originally designed in teak with a maple monogram, has handles hand carved of teak, which become an integral part with the bottom.

The bottom is made of ¼-inch plywood, the sides curved to an 18-inch radius. The top and bottom are veneered, the top inlaid with a large monogram. The longer sides are rabbeted top and bottom to leave a tongue ⅛ inch by ⅛ inch for attaching the sides. The ends are rabbeted to form a tongue ⅛ inch thick by ¼ inch long to

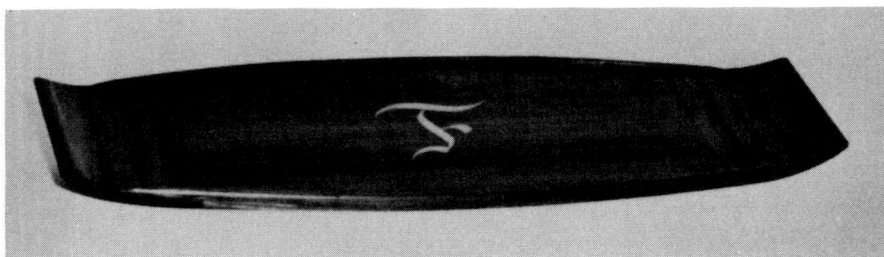

Small serving tray

Number of Pieces	Size	Description
1	$\frac{1}{4}'' \times 8'' \times 20\frac{1}{2}''$	Plywood tray bottom
2	$\frac{3}{4}'' \times 4'' \times 6\frac{5}{8}''$	Hardwood handles
2	$\frac{1}{4}'' \times \frac{1}{2}'' \times 24''$	Hardwood sides
2	$\frac{1}{28}'' \times 8\frac{1}{4}'' \times 20''$	Hardwood veneer

Piece of veneer for monogram

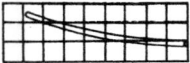

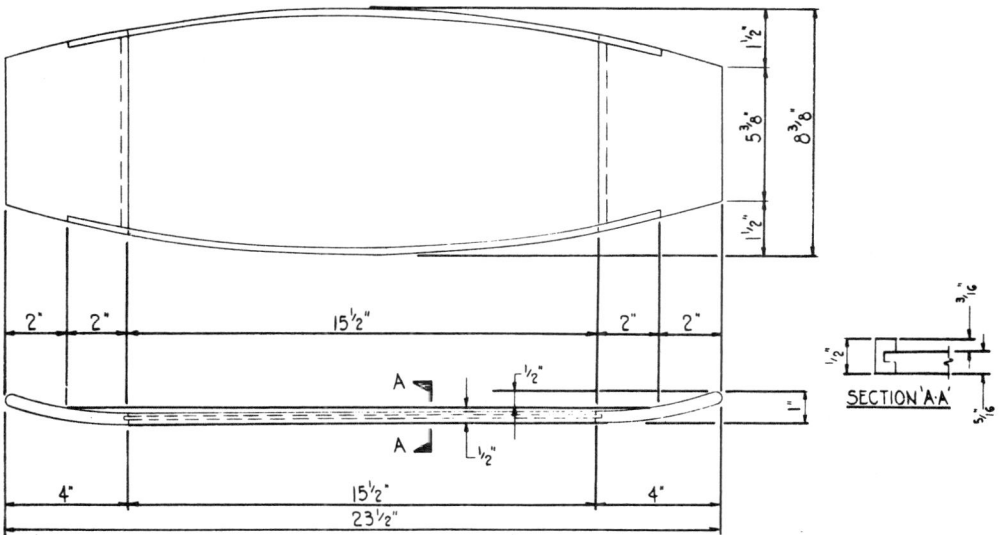

Small serving tray

attach the handles. Sand the top face before assembly.

Enlarge the pattern for the handle curves and transfer to both ends of the handles. The pattern should touch the corners of the wood at each end to minimize the amount of carving necessary. Bevel the inside edge of the handle 10°. Make a $\frac{1}{8}$-inch-by-$\frac{1}{4}$-inch-deep groove in the beveled edge, in a position to allow the bottom of the handle to be flush with the veneered bottom. Measure the location of the groove from the bottom of the tray.

With wood-carving gouges and coarse abrasive paper, chisel and shape the curve of the top of the handle across the wood until the lines at each end are reached. The curve on the bottom of the handle is shaped with a small plane and abrasive paper. Do not remove too much wood near the grooved edge or the handle and veneer will not match. After shaping cut the handles to the proper width using the curve of the 18-inch radius. Round the edge of the end of the handle. Glue the handles to the tray making sure they are centered. The handles should be ⅛ inch wider than the tray at both ends.

The side pieces are cut to length and slightly wider than the finished width. Groove ⅛ inch by ⅛ inch so that $^3/_{16}$ inch projects above the top of the tray. Round the top edge. The bottom of the strips must be cut away where the handles meet the tray. Make a vertical saw cut with a coping saw about two inches from either end. Measure carefully before cutting. The fitting of the two inches on each end is done with a sharp knife carving until the underside of the trim butts the curve of the handles.

Glue the trim and clamp with bar clamps near the ends of the grooved portion with tapered scraps of softwood between the clamp and edging to compensate for the curve. Clamp the ends to the handles with small C-clamps with thin pieces of wood inserted to prevent warping of the tray. Glue all joints with waterproof glue.

Trim and sand all solid wood flush. Remove any excess glue and sand the tray smooth.

Finish with an alcohol-resistant finish.

14 Decorative Switch Plates

The switch plates shown in the drawing are only two of an infinite variety possible. A favorite shape can be taken from ceramic tile, a pattern used in a room, or a cartoon character for a child's room. The latter could be enameled or made from veneers as inlays or overlays. The plates may be made regular or irregular in shape. They may be centered or off center, but make them large enough and in a position to protect the walls around the switch from finger marks.

After deciding upon the design, cut the plate from ¼-inch hardwood. Use the plastic switch plate cover you are replacing to mark the cutouts for the switches and the holes for the screws. Place the outer surface of the plastic against the wood for greater accuracy when marking, as the plastic will be against the wood.

Drill and countersink the screw holes and cut the rectangular openings for the switches with a jigsaw or coping saw. File the

Decorative switch plates

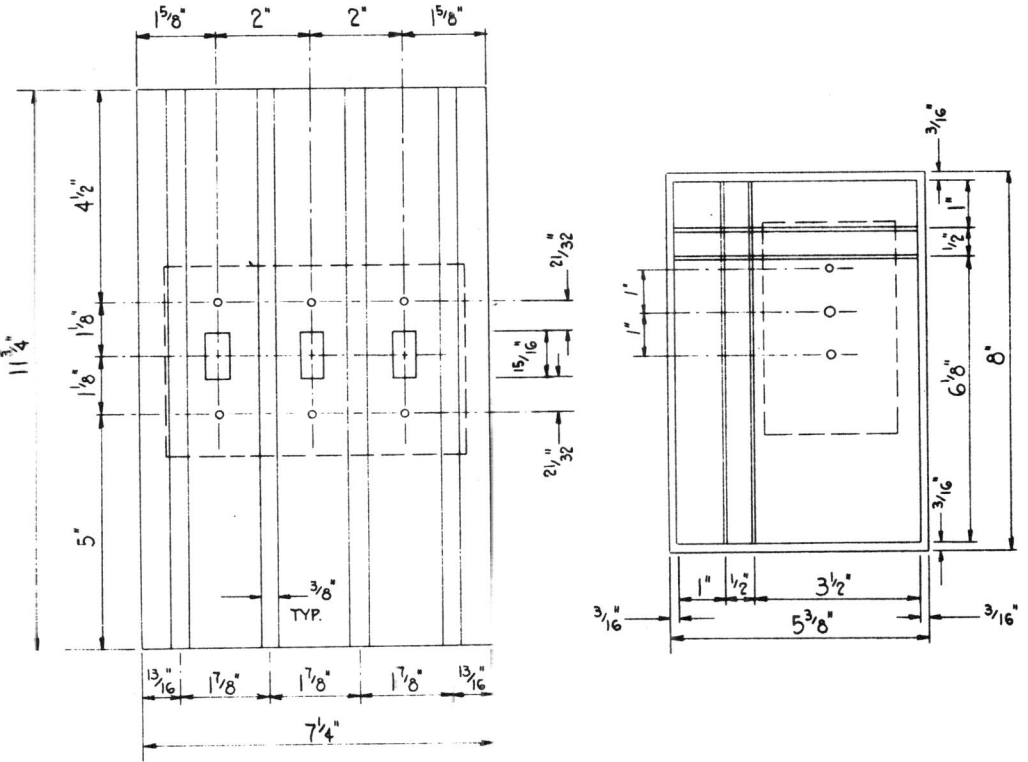

Decorative switch plates

openings to the outside edge of the lines to prevent binding of the wood and switches when installing. Round or bevel the edges for a more finished appearance. Saw or rout any desired grooves, but limit their depth to $1/16$ inch.

Cut a $1/16$-inch-deep recess in the back over the area which will cover the electrical box in the wall. Glue asbestos paper in this area.

Finish the wood in a finish which will match the room. If light-colored wood is used, it may be stained with one of the new colored stains to match colors in the room. Glue chrome mylar in the grooves if desired.

Install the switch plates using the screws from the plastic plate being replaced. If the screwheads do not match, leave the screws protruding slightly and paint the heads with a small brush. Tighten after the paint dries.

15 Pipe Rack

Cherry and ebony were used for this unusual design. The ebony is sandwiched between cherry to form a stripe in the edge of the parabolic support.

Pipe rack

Number of Pieces	Size	Description
2	½″× 4½″× 10¾″	Hardwood
2	¼″× 2″×5″	Hardwood, supports
2	⅛″× 3″×3″	Hardwood upper supports
1	⅛″× 2″×5″	Hardwood, supports
1	⅛″× 3″×3″	Hardwood upper supports
	⅛″	Dowel

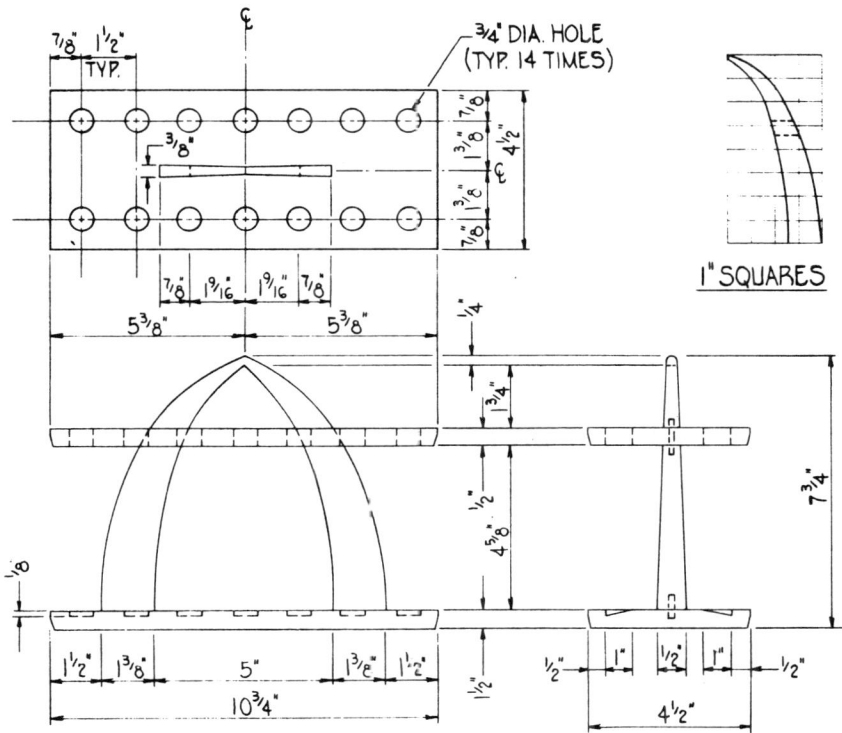

Pipe rack

The top and bottom are cut to size from ½-inch cherry. The lower ⅜ inch of the edges are slightly beveled (about 5°) on the table saw. Holes ¾ inch in diameter are drilled in the top as shown in the drawing. Clamp scrap wood to the back of the top to prevent splintering when drilling.

The recesses for the pipe bowls are cut with a ¾-inch wood-carvers gouge. Take small bites of wood when cutting and keep the gouge sharp to prevent splintering. A straight chisel or knife is used to true up the vertical walls of the recesses.

Glue a piece of ⅛-inch ebony between two pieces of ¼-inch cherry to make up the wood for the lower supports. Glue ⅛-inch ebony between ⅛-inch cherry for the upper part of the support. Enlarge the pattern for the support and cut out the portion between the dotted lines, which is the thickness of the top. Saw two pieces for the lower supports from the thicker laminated stock and two upper pieces from the thinner stock. Plane and file the lower supports to taper from ½ inch at the bottom to ⅜ inch at the top. Shape to an elongated oval cross section. The top pieces are tapered ⅜ inch at the bottom to ¼ inch at the top where the piece joins the member from the other side. The cross-section shape is oval at the bottom to round at the top. Leave the final shaping of the top until after assembly.

Locate the position of the bottom supports on the base and drill matching ⅛-inch holes in the supports and base for ⅛-inch dowels. Similarly locate holes at the top of the support and the underside of the top.

Sand all pieces before assembly.

Glue the top, base, and supports with a strong glue, weighting the top while the glue dries.

Locate holes for ⅛-inch dowels in the bottom of the upper members of the parabolic support and the top surface of the rack. The joint at the top of the parabola is fastened with glue alone. The top joint cannot be clamped and is held with tape while the glue hardens. The completed top shape is finished and cemented to place.

The original was finished with a satin finish sealer and wax.

16 Veneered Clock

The face of the clock is made of wedge-shaped pieces of hardwood veneers in place of numbers. In the arrangement shown, the junction of the veneered wedges and the points of the walnut border trim is the position of the numbers.

A clock movement which runs on 110-volt current is needed to turn the oversize hands, which are made from medium weight sheet brass. If a battery operated movement is to be used, it would be best to reduce the size of the clock to be compatible with the recommended size hands.

Start construction by laying out the twelve-sided face on ¼-inch plywood. Draw vertical and horizontal midlines. Mark the 4¾-inch-long sides at 3, 6, 9 and 12 o'clock with the midlines as their center. Lay out the remaining sides 30° from the ends of each of the four

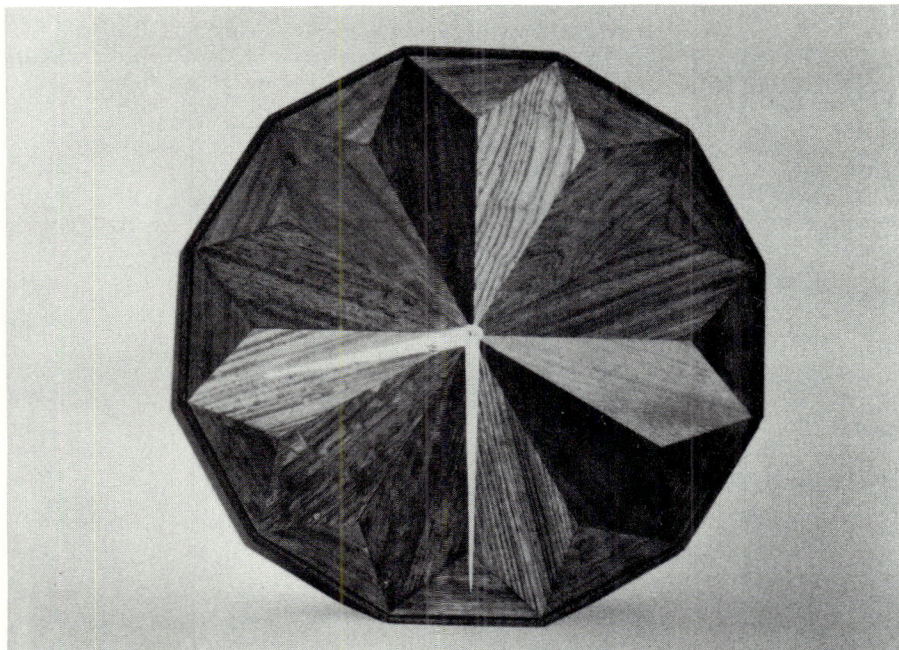

Veneered clock

original sides. Saw the plywood to shape and bevel the edge of each side 30°.

Draw a radius 30° to one midline to the edge of the clock face. Cut a cardboard pattern of this segment to cut the veneer. Cut the veneer segments accurately and slightly longer than the pattern. Use veneers that contrast and tape to form the panel with the colors arranged for maximum contrast.

Glue the veneer panel to the plywood with contact cement. There is no room for error here, as the center of the veneer must be at the center of the plywood. Drill a small hole at the center of the veneer panel. Tap a nail into the center of the plywood and remove. After coating veneer and plywood with cement, cover the plywood with two pieces of brown wrapping paper, one piece on either side of the midline. Place the veneer on the paper and insert the nail through the veneer into the hole in the plywood. Line up one of the joints between the veneer with a midline, remove one sheet of paper at a time and glue.

Trim excess veneer from the edges of the panel, drill the hole in the center for the clock movement, and sand.

Cut the twelve ¼-inch walnut sides. Use a table of angles to set the

Number of Pieces	Size	Description
1	¼″× 18″×18″	Plywood
12	¼″× 4⅞″×3½″	Walnut
12	Varied wood veneers	
	1 sq. ft.	Walnut veneer
1	1½″× 1½″×2½″	Softwood
	.020 sheet brass	Hands

Clock movement

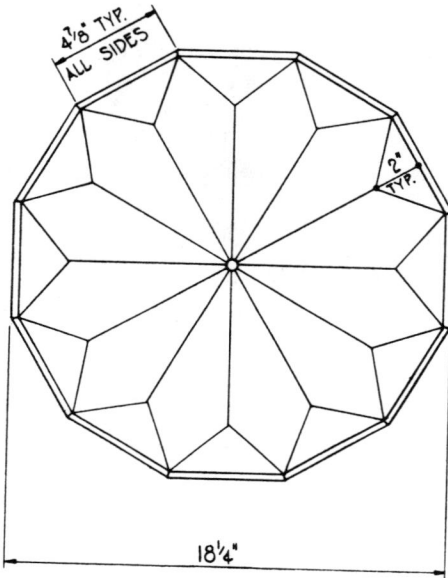

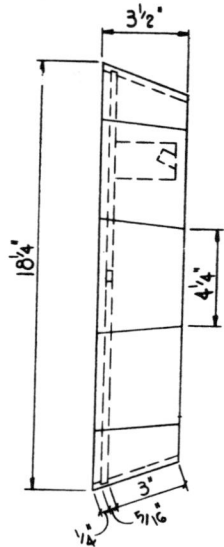

Veneered clock

blade tilt and miter gauge to make the cuts for a twelve-sided box. Lacking the table, cut the pieces 4⅞″ in front and 4¼″ in back. After cutting bevel the sides 15°.

Cut a ⁵⁄₁₆-inch-wide groove ⅛ inch from the front edge in each side with the saw tilted 30°. Use a dado blade or make repeated passes with a saw blade.

Sand the ¼ inch of wood foreward of the groove in the sides before assembly.

Trial assemble the pieces before gluing. Make adjustments in the miters with a file and sandpaper on a sanding block until everything fits perfectly.

Glue the sides of the clock face and to each other and clamp with a band clamp.

Cut triangles of walnut veneer 4¾ inches at the base with the other two sides meeting at the apex 2 inches from the base. Mark the positions of the triangles on the clock face with a sharp pencil. Sand the faces of the triangles and glue to place with contact cement being careful not to paint the cement outside the lines drawn on the clock face.

Glue a softwood block inside in the position shown for hanging the clock. Drill a ¼-inch hole into the block at an angle for hanging. A large nail driven into the wall at an angle is used for hanging.

Sand the walnut trim and finish with a boiled linseed oil finish.

If the clock is constructed the size shown, make the hands from sheet brass about .020 inch thick. The hour hand is 7 inches long and the minute hand 8½ inches long. They should be wide enough at the movement end to accommodate the hole for installation without breaking, tapering to ⅛ inch at the top.

17 Stack Tables

The three tables have walnut veneered tops and solid walnut legs. Striped walnut veneer was used in order to match the grain at two joints.

The tops are equilateral triangles with the corners rounded making

Stack tables

Number of Pieces	Size	Description
3	¾″× 18″ triangle	Plywood top
9	¾″× 6″×16¼″	Hardwood legs
	8 sq. ft.	Veneer
9	#6	Wood screws
	¼″	Dowel or finishing nails

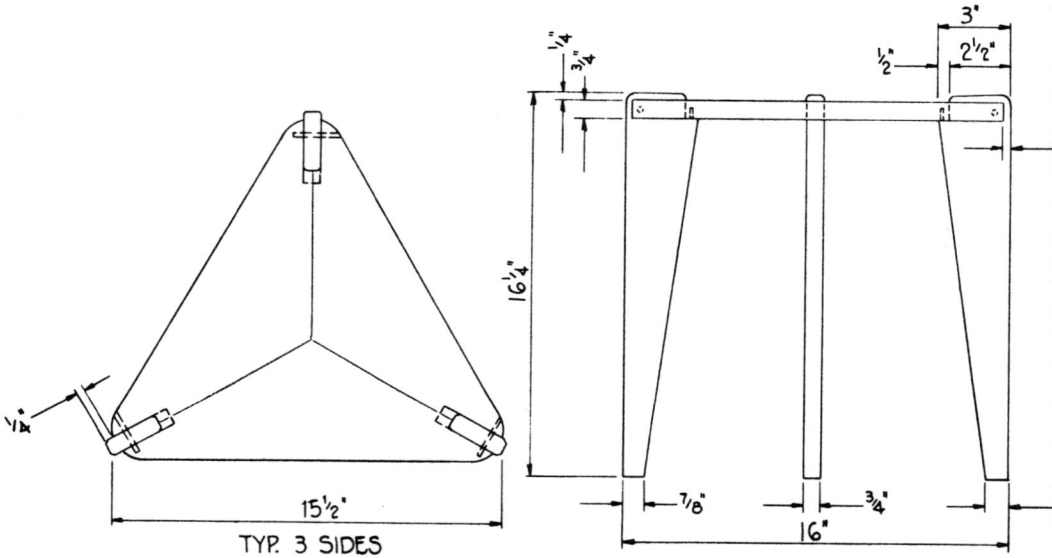

TYP. 3 SIDES

Stack tables

each side 16 inches. Before rounding the corners draw lines from each apex to the middle of the side opposite. These lines are the midlines of the notches for the legs. Notches ¾ inch wide by 2¼ inch long are cut in each corner.

Make a cardboard pattern of a table segment (area between two lines and one side of the table) to aid in cutting the veneers leaving excess at the table edges. Glue the veneer to the table tops, trim excess from the edges, and cut the veneer from the notches.

The legs are cut to the dimensions shown. The taper is cut on the inner part of the leg only, so two legs may be cut from a board 6 inches wide to save wood. Notch the inner angle at the top ½ inch by 1 inch and round the edges to ¼ inch radius. If a router is used, round cross-grain areas at the top before the sides of the legs to prevent any splintering of wood at the end of the cut. If the edge is being shaped

84

with hand tools, use a plane with the grain and a file across the grain. Finish shaping with medium abrasive paper.

Sand all parts before assembly and cut veneer strips for the table edges.

The legs are fastened with a ¼-inch dowel or finishing nail driven across the ends of the top through the leg as shown. Hold the leg in position in its notch with the table top upside down on the workbench. Place a piece of ¼-inch wood under the end opposite the leg to support the top perpendicular to the leg. Drill a ¼-inch hole as shown if a dowel is used, glue the dowel and notch, and drive the dowel to place. When the glue dries cut the dowel flush with the side. If a nail is used, drill the hole slightly smaller than the finishing nail used through one part of the top and through the leg. Glue the notch and hammer the nail to place flush with the side. Drill a counterbored hole in the inner portion of the leg and screw to the top.

Veneer the edges using contact cement. Bar clamps with light pressure may be needed to hold down the curved ends of the veneer, if they spring away from the table edge.

Finish by sanding and use a boiled linseed oil finish.

18   Pipe Rack and Humidor

This pipe rack was originally made of Brazilian rosewood. Beveled edges were used for the original pictured, but squared edges are more pleasing in modern design.

Cut the base and top of the pipe rack from solid hardwood. If ⅝-inch wood is unavailable, use ½-inch-thick stock or have thicker wood surfaced to ⅝ inch. Lay out the positions of the ¾-inch holes on the top and the recesses in the same position on the base. Clamp scrap wood in back of the top when drilling to prevent splintering. Cut the tapered recesses in the base with a sharp wood-carver's gouge. The front walls of the recesses are squared with a sharp chisel or knife.

Rout a recess ⅛ inch deep at the end of the base for the humidor.

Lay out the support from two pieces of hardwood using a ruler and protractor. Cut the pieces and glue and dowel the miter.

Sand all pieces and glue the top to the support with a strong glue. Fasten the lower end of the support to the base with glue and a 1-inch #8 flathead wood screw. Make a countersunk hole in the base to allow the screw to be flush. A pilot hole drilled in the bottom of the support will prevent splitting. Make sure the two parts are aligned before the glue dries.

Pipe rack and humidor

Bill of Materials

Number of Pieces	Size	Description
1	⅝″× 6″×14½″	Hardwood, base
1	⅝″× 6″×9″	Hardwood, top
2 pieces		Hardwood, support
2	¼″× 5″×6⅛″	Plywood, sides
2	¼″×4½″×6⅛″	Plywood, sides
2	¼″×4½″×4½″	Plywood, top & bottom
1½ sq. ft.		Veneer
1	⅛″× ⅝″×20″	Plywood, lip of lid

Construct the humidor of ¼-inch plywood. To ensure that the lid is identical in size make the lid and box as one unit and saw the lid using a fine blade on a table saw. Nail and glue the sides of the box and the ends. Cut the veneer for the sides and glue successive pieces matching the wood grain around the box. Veneer the top and sand smooth. Saw the lid (veneered end) from the box and glue strips of ⅛-inch plywood to the inside of the lid to form a lip on the inside. Round or chamfer the outer edge of the lip to allow the cover to slide into place easily.

Finish with a boiled linseed oil finish or sealer for a satin finish. Paint or varnish the inside of the humidor to prevent absorption of moisture. Store tobacco in a closed plastic bag for ease of handling and to prevent drying out.

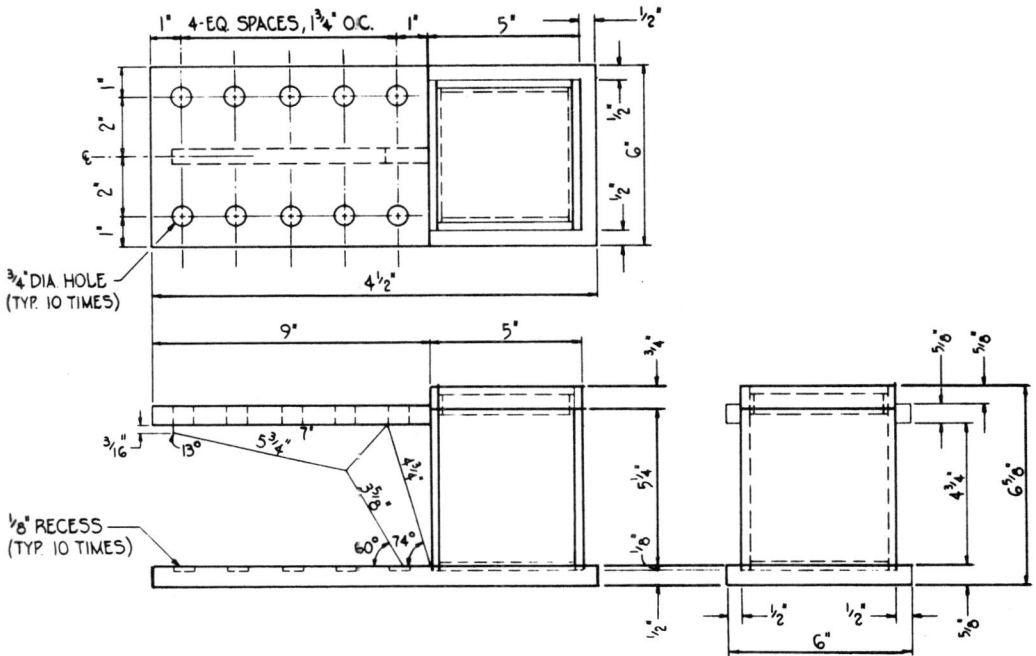

Pipe rack and humidor

19 Parquet Parson's Table

The table shown is the size of an end or lamp table made with a walnut veneered top and solid walnut legs and rails. If dimensions must be changed, design the veneered panel first so the squares will be the same size.

Walnut 1½-inch square was used for the legs and 1½ inch by 2¼ inch for the rails. Cut the four legs and tenon the top removing ½ inch of stock from two adjacent sides making the tenon 1 inch square and 1 inch long.

Cut the rails to length mitering the ends 45°. Rabbet the inner part of the rails ¾ inch wide and slightly less than ¹³/₁₆ inch deep for the veneered plywood top. Glue the rails with urea resin or resorcin resin glue clamping with four bar clamps, two lengthwise and two across the width. A band clamp may be used if one is available.

Form one-inch-square mortises 1 inch deep, ½ inch from each outer edge in the underside of the rails. If a drill press and mortising chisel

87

Parquet parson's table

BILL OF MATERIALS

Number of Pieces	Size	Description
4	1½"× 1½"× 19¼"	Hardwood, legs
2	1½"×2¼"×27½"	Hardwood long rails
2	1½"×2¼"× 17"	Hardwood short rails
1	¾"× 14"×24½"	Plywood, top
	2½ sq. ft.	Veneer, top
8	2½" #8	Flathead wood screws
10	1¼" #8	Flathead wood screws

are unavailable use a router with a ¼-inch-diameter straight bit and round the corners of the tenons to match the mortises. Adjust the tenons so the joint doesn't bind when assembled or the joints in the rails may open when the legs are glued.

Attach the legs to one end of the table at a time. The top is placed upside down overhanging the workbench and the legs are clamped in their mortises. When the legs are square with the rails, drill pilot holes for screws from the inner face of each rail adjacent the leg into the tenon. Glue the joint with resorcin resin, clamp the legs, square, and screw with two 2½-inch #8 flathead wood screws. After the glue hardens unclamp and assemble the other legs.

88

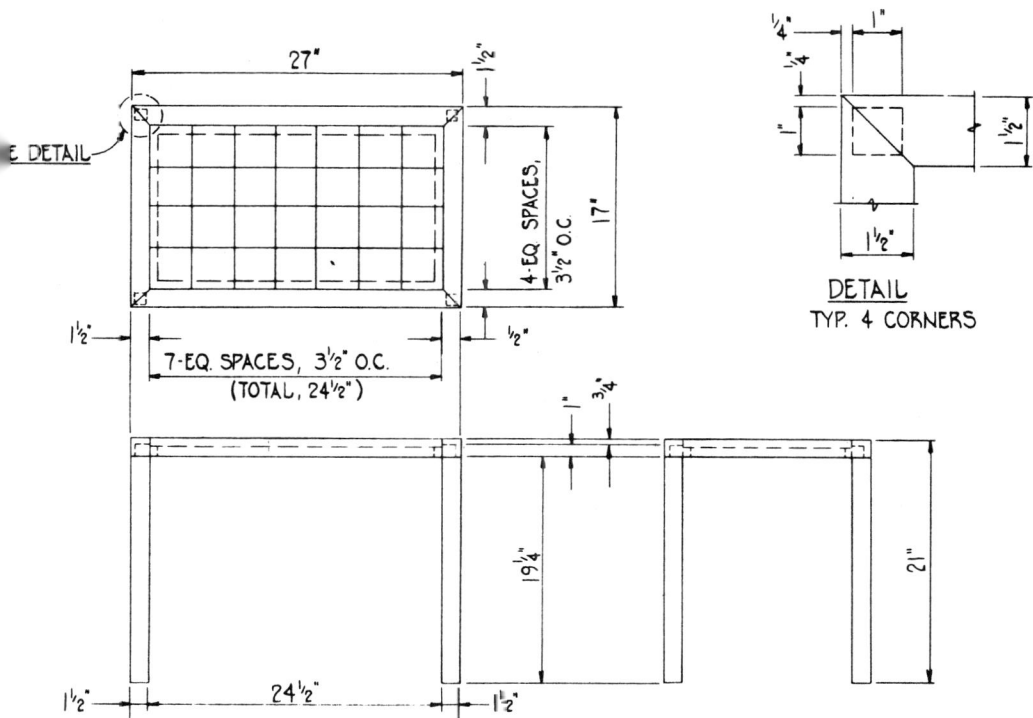

Parquet parson's table

Cut ¾-inch plywood for the top to fit exactly between the rails. Cut 3½-inch squares of walnut veneer for the parquet top and tape into a panel with the grain at right angles to the grain of the adjacent square. Make the outer squares oversize in case the panel is not glued in perfect alignment. Glue the panel and trim the excess veneer.

Insert the veneered top in the rabbet. Do not force to place. Plane any spots that bind. If the veneer is above the top of the rails, the rabbet must be made deeper using a router. If the rails are slightly higher, sand level after attaching the top.

Drill countersunk holes from the bottom and screw the top in place with 1¼-inch #8 flathead wood screws. Use three screws on the long sides and two in short.

Fill any slight voids in the joints with matching wood filler, sand thoroughly, and finish with boiled linseed oil or wax finish.

Appendix: Suppliers

Craftsman Wood Service Company
1735 Cortland Ct.
Addison, Illinois 60101

Albert Constantine and Son, Inc.
2050 Eastchester Road
Bronx, New York 10461

Glossary

ALIPHATIC RESIN GLUE. *See* YELLOW GLUE.

BAND CLAMP. A clamping device that utilizes a nylon band for clamping irregular objects.

BAR CLAMP. A clamping device with a long bar used to clamp the edges of wood when gluing panels or corners of boxes during assembly.

BITS. Boring tools of varying diameters used with a brace.

BLOCK PLANE. A small plane for smoothing across the end grain of wood.

BOOK MATCH. The matching of adjacent sheets of veneer in a flitch so that one sheet appears to be the mirror image of the other.

BRACE. A crank-shaped tool with handles and a chuck for holding wood-cutting bits.

BURL FIGURE. Wood pattern found in growths on the trunk or limbs of trees.

BUTT FIGURE. Pattern of woodgrain found in wood cut from the stump of a tree.

BUTT JOINT. A joint made by fastening wood end to end or edge to edge without overlap.

CAUL. Heavy pieces of wood used to distribute pressure when clamping large panels of wood.

C-CLAMP. A steel-framed clamp shaped like the letter *C* for clamping small objects.

CHISEL, WOOD. A flat metal tool with a sharpened edge for chipping, carving, or shaving wood.

COMPOUND MITER. A miter joint that incorporates a bevel.

CONTACT CEMENT. A solvent-based cement that is applied to both surfaces to be joined and allowed to dry. Adhesion is immediate upon contact of the two surfaces.

COPING SAW. A saw with a U-shaped frame for holding thin, narrow saw blades. Used for sawing intricate cuts.

CROTCH. Pattern found in the wood taken from the section just below the fork of the tree.

DADO. A groove cut in the edge, end, or face of a board.

DIAMOND MATCH. The matching of striped veneers to form a diamond-shaped pattern.

DISK SANDER. A fixed power tool with a circular abrasive disk or an attachment for an electric drill usually used to sand the edges or ends of wood.

EPOXY CEMENT. A two-art resin glue that yields a very strong joint.

FIGURED VENEERS. Veneers cut from a portion of the tree where the grain pattern is distorted.

FILE, WOOD. A hardened steel tool with sharpened edges used to shape and smooth wood.

FLITCH. A complete package of veneer with sheets in sequence as they are sliced or sawn from the log.

FRAMING SQUARE. A large measuring tool with two straight edges at right angles.

HARDWOOD. Wood from a broad-leafed tree.

INLAY. A piece of wood or other material set into another background piece of wood.

JACK PLANE. A large plane for truing wood surfaces. Used in the direction of the grain of the wood.

JIG SAW. A stationary power saw with a narrow, thin blade for sawing intricate cuts.

JOINTING. The process of truing a joint, usually by planing.

MITER JOINT. A joint made by fastening parts at right angles by means of a bevel.

NAIL SET. An elongated instrument with a dull point for driving headless nails below the surface of wood.

ORBITAL SANDER. A portable power sander which moves abrasive paper in an arc. Used for sanding the face of wood.

PIPE CLAMP. Similar to a bar clamp, but using a length of pipe instead of a steel bar.

POLYVINYL GLUE. *See* WHITE GLUE.

RABBET. A groove cut in the face of a board at its edge or end.

RABBET JOINT. A joint formed by fastening a board in a groove at the edge or end of another board.

RESORCIN RESIN GLUE. A two-part powder-and-liquid glue that yields a waterproof joint.

92

SABER SAW. A portable power saw with narrow, thin blades for making intricate cuts.

SANDING BLOCK. A flat block of hardwood or other material around which abrasive paper is held when sanding wood.

SOFTWOOD. Wood from a coniferous tree.

SPLINE. A thin wood strip glued into a groove in a joint for strength.

SPRING CLAMP. A clothespinlike metal clamp for holding small objects.

TABLE SAW. A large power saw with a circular blade used for sawing straight, bevel, and miter cuts. Also called a circular saw.

TAC RAG. A rag, usually cheesecloth, impregnated with varnish andd linseed oil, used to pick up dust before applying finishes.

TRY SQUARE. A measuring tool with two straight edges fastened at right angles. One edge is used for measuring.

VENEER. A thin layer of wood or other material.

VENEER SAW. A thin-bladed, short-handled saw for cutting wood veneer.

VENEER TAPE. Gummed paper tape used to hold veneer pieces together.

WHITE GLUE. Polyvinyl glue in ready-to-use form for general gluing where a waterproof bond is not required.

YELLOW GLUE. Aliphatic resin glue similar to polyvinyl but stronger.

Bibliography

Feirer, John L. *Cabinetmaking and Millwork.* Peoria, Ill.: Charles A. Bennett Co., Inc., 1967

Hjorth, Herman. *Veneering Made Easy.* New York: Albert Constantine and Son, Inc., 1961.

Holbrook, Wallace. *Contemporary Lamps.* Bloomington, Ill.: McKnight and McKnight, 1968.

Index